TALES OF AN AMERICAN HOBO

SINGULAR LIVES

The Iowa Series in North American Autobiography

Albert E. Stone, Series Editor

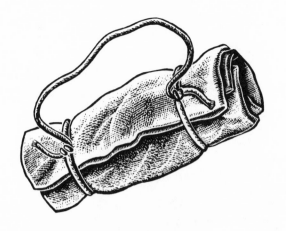

TALES OF AN

AMERICAN HOBO

BY CHARLES ELMER FOX

PREFACE BY ALBERT E. STONE

INTRODUCTION BY
LYNNE M. ADRIAN

UNIVERSITY OF IOWA PRESS

IOWA CITY

Ψ

University of Iowa Press, Iowa City 52242
Copyright © 1989 by the University of Iowa
All rights reserved
Printed in the United States of America
First edition, 1989

Design by Sandra Strother Hudson
Wood engravings by Beth Krommes
Typesetting by G&S Typesetters, Austin, Texas
Printing and binding by Edwards Brothers,
Ann Arbor, Michigan

Library of Congress
Cataloging-in-Publication Data
Fox, Charles Elmer.
    Tales of an American hobo/by Charles Elmer
Fox; preface by Albert E. Stone; introduction by
Lynne M. Adrian.—1st ed.
        p.   cm.—(Singular lives)
    ISBN 0-87745-251-2, ISBN 0-87745-252-0
(pbk.)
    1. Fox, Charles Elmer.   2. Tramps—United
States—Biography.   I. Title.   II. Series.
HV4505.F68   1989
305.5′68—dc20   89-5055
[B]   CIP

Printed on acid-free paper

IN MEMORY OF THEM ALL

Boxcars rattling in the rain,
The age-old song of a speeding train.
It takes me back to the long ago,
To Mulligan Shorty and Bug-eyed Joe.

I've sat with them by many fires,
When the days came to an end,
And heard a steam train whistle moan
As she came around the bend.

Off on some distant mountain grade
In the wee hours of the night,
The cracking exhaust of a steamer at work
And her piercing yellow light.

As the embers of the fire glow faintly
And the long hours of night pass on,
I think of old friends and the steamers I loved,
For all are now dead and gone.

       —Charles Elmer Fox

CONTENTS

PREFACE

"Reefer Charlie" Fox is the second autobiographer to appear in the University of Iowa Press' Singular Lives series. Like his predecessor's inaugural volume, Milt Felsen's *The Anti-Warrior: A Memoir*, Fox's *Tales of an American Hobo* was written late in an active, ongoing life. It also joins as a late contribution a sizable body of similarly inspired stories written out of social experiences long past, forgotten by many or even unknown to them. As Lynne Adrian points out in her introduction, however, American readers for more than a century have vicariously enjoyed the adventures and mishaps (more or less authenticated) of the "knights of the road." The popularity of such unconventional autobiographies has risen and fallen as concern for an endemic social problem has given way to a more comfortable nostalgia and historical curiosity and as the railroad has declined in economic and cultural significance. But while today's detective novels and films continue to exploit the excitement and glamor still attached to railroad travel—in first class, at least, the ideal setting for mystery and romance—so, too, there persists a fascination with those who once rode the rods beneath the dining cars and plush compartments where Hitchcock's heroines and villains enact their timeless deceptions. "I'm the last of a kind," Fox announces (prematurely, we hope) of his place in our social annals. In fact, a prime aim of his richly anecdotal account is to memorialize a past world and his dead pals who "have caught that westbound freight." In the process, Reefer Charlie does more than recall the characters and life-style of his peers and predecessors. He leaves us an indelible sketch of his own personality and onetime position in the hobo society once flourishing, often unnoticed, along our highways and roadbeds.

As social historian and self-portraitist, Fox both follows and enriches the tradition marked earlier in the century by such best-sellers as *Life and Adventures of A No. One: America's Most Celebrated Tramp, Written by Himself* and its more unusual variant, *Sister of the Road: The Autobiography of Boxcar Bertha*. Unlike many of his predecessors, Fox is seldom the muckraker intent on using his life story as a political tool to expose social ills and criminal riffraff. *Tales of an American Hobo* is more an idealist's version of and apology for hobohemia, one in which the upper crust of the vagabond battalions are shown to be living by a "jungle law" as respectable and moral as that of the settled citizenry and more admirable than the common mores of the tramps and bums from whom Fox carefully distances himself and his hobo brethren. "Hoboes will work, tramps won't, and bums can't" is his wording of the usual distinction. The hoboes Charlie has known and admired often got their start, he admits, as tramps and bums. They all share itchy feet and a detestation of regimentation. But many of his friends, like the aging vegetarian who teaches Charlie the virtues of a fruit diet, steal only to eat or keep warm. They are somewhat less racially prejudiced than others on the road, where the lot of blacks and Mexicans was little better than in the settlements. Moreover, Fox is discreet about the prevalence of homosexuality in the jungles and boxcars of the past.

American social history, as documented by this amateur expert, is enriched by fresh insights, facts, and value judgments coming "from below." "The road is a constant source of knowledge to those who have an open mind," Fox writes. Hoboes share what amounts to a distinct subculture characterized by a shared vocabulary, work skills and recreation habits, folklore and superstitions, and even an institutional structure quite similar to sections of the dominant society. Relationships with the larger society are, however, chiefly antagonistic inasmuch as they are usually defined by unfriendly judges, railroad dicks, and brakeys. Nevertheless, Fox argues that by contrast with ordinary social standards Crabb Switch, a modern hobo jungle, is almost an ideal social community. Moreover, his account of his strategies for feeding surplus food to a whole group of homeless is a parable of public service and shrewdness.

Such events, insights, and personal relationships recalled from the years between the wars form the content of these somewhat random anecdotes and informal lectures. Each episode contributes to an increasingly convincing picture of Charlie Fox's engaging personality. By the story's end, he stands clear as a cheerful, optimistic, fast-talking, and quick-witted man with enough raw courage to serve him well in emergencies. "I can only get so scared," he tells one murderous escapee from the penitentiary who threatens his life; "then I get a little dangerous." His pocketknife backs up these brave words. Other aspects of his decency are revealed as he identifies the heroes remembered from years on the road. Besides the old vegetarian mentioned above, he memorializes the fair-minded town marshal of Pacific Junction, Iowa, and Soup Bean Annie of Sparks, Nevada. The policeman, praising Charlie and his companion for crossing the flooding Missouri on a railroad trestle, sends them on their way, well supplied, across Iowa. Annie is remembered for always keeping a large soup pot on the kitchen stove to serve hoboes and other wanderers as she waits for her hobo husband to return.

Such modest but telling vignettes of obscure Americans and their hitherto undocumented lives constitute the special gift of this warmhearted memoir. Charlie Fox and his late-appearing account of life on the road may never match the fame of "A No. 1," Jim Tully, or Jack London. But few amateur writers have left more appealing or richer records of the everyday lives of ordinary Americans: the train-hopping, homeless migratory workers who for over a century maintained a distinctive way of life. It is one from which we nine-to-five readers may learn much.

ALBERT E. STONE

INTRODUCTION

Many contemporary scholars maintain that we cannot recover the views, the life experiences, and the beliefs of America's hoboes because hoboes were an inarticulate population. I suspect that, because they have never met Charlie Fox, they believe that we can't know how hoboes thought. There is nothing inarticulate about Charlie, either in person or in print, yet there is none of the upper-middle-class, educated adventurer exploring life on the road about Charlie, either. As he has proudly told me many times, his higher education was a correspondence course with the Palmer Institute of Authorship, North Hollywood, and his graduate degree was a 100 percent welding certificate. Charlie gained the rest of his knowledge in what my father calls the "school of hard knocks." While many of the knocks *were* hard in road life, there was also much beauty and worth, and Charlie conveys both in simple, direct prose that is as surely American as Walt Whitman's— though Charlie's own poetry is written more in the style of John Greenleaf Whittier.

In the 1890s a distinct hobo subculture emerged within America's working class. As America industrialized, there was a huge need to create an infrastructure of railroads, bridges, commercial one-crop agriculture, and even new towns out west that would serve as an economic base for the growing cities and their manufacturing. Not only were workers needed to lay and repair railroad track, build bridges, and harvest grain, but those activities created a need for lumber and iron ore to build the tracks and machines, creating even more jobs in unsettled areas. Much of the work was both necessary and inherently temporary. Who was to fill such a vital labor market niche? Most newly arriving immigrants settled in cities, and because the need for mobility meant a need for fluent English, the work was left to American-born workers or immigrants from the British Isles; in short, to hoboes. And despite the fact that contemporary social reformers could not see it, there is no question that hoboes were workers; indeed, as Charlie once remarked, "Who else but a hobo would travel a thousand miles to make a dollar a day harvesting wheat?"

Hoboes, then, were English-speaking migratory workers. They were also almost always young and unmarried. At a time when as much as 30 percent of American men were bachelors, hoboes evolved a distinct subculture with its own language, skills (it is *not* easy to hop a freight train!), rules of behavior, and even "hobohemia" areas of many cities where they stayed between jobs or went to find new ones. For some hoboing was a disaster: injuries on the road or demoralizing jobs with working conditions so bad that three crews were hired—one coming, one going, one working—produced the down and out "homeguard" of what later became the nation's skid rows. For most, however, hoboing was a youthful stage, a kind of working-class Grand Tour, with opportunities for experience, adventure, and manly independence from the constraints of factory life, a phase to be ended only when a special place (or person) created a pull to settle down that was as strong as the pull the wanderlust created to travel the rails. And that experience is what Charlie Fox chronicles.

To the vast majority of Americans, the men who came to beg food at back doors were as likely to be classified as "no good bums" or tramps or vagrants as they were to be called hoboes. To the respectable residents of small-town America there was no difference. To the men who were "throwing their feet" asking for a handout, there were important distinctions among hobo, tramp, and bum. In the argot of the road "a hobo was someone who travelled and worked, a tramp was someone who travelled but didn't work, and a bum was someone who didn't travel and didn't work."[1] These distinctions point out two very important facts. First, the image of the wanderer in the public mind is greatly over-simplified. He is seen either as a romantic figure following the open road—a paragon of Emerson's self-reliance—or as a parasite on society, an apostate of Franklin's faith in industriousness and civic virtue. Second, hoboes frequently responded to the popular stereotype of wanderers as lazy by distinguishing themselves—at least in their own parlance—from those who did not work.

Another common stereotype about America's wanderers was that they were ignorant and illiterate. This stereotype is as untrue as the assumption that they are lazy. It is belied by the *Hobo News* (later retitled *Hobo World*), published from about 1900 until about 1937, a monthly magazine containing articles, short stories, and poems written and edited by hoboes themselves.[2] It is also refuted by a whole subgenre of approximately forty hobo autobiographies, most written between 1880 and 1940. Almost invariably they were written after their authors had ceased actively riding the rails. Given the physical activity necessary in hoboing, this fact is not surprising. While all are backward glances, either to the immediate or the distant past, the degree to which they are merely nostalgic rather than self-revelatory varies greatly. In Charlie Fox's *Tales of an American Hobo*, perhaps more than in any other manuscript, nostalgia is at a minimum. What emerges instead is a clear picture of "Reefer Charlie" as an individual and hoboes as members of a wandering subculture.

Like these other autobiographies, however, Charlie's includes certain persisting elements. All the hobo autobiographies tell of the author's first train ride and the hobo who initiated him (or rarely her) into the ways of the road. The autobiographies include stories of decking a fast train, holding down a particularly hard train, or riding in a tough spot on the train. They include a tale of an unusual person who has taught the author something important and the tale of someone killed from riding a train the wrong way. There are tales of the beauties of nature, run-ins with the law, and developing skill at begging for food (in Charlie's case, enough skill to feed an entire neighborhood during the Depression). These tales have a great significance in the subculture. In a sense they are fossilized folktales—common life experiences preserved in the amber of individual recollection. They are part of a hobo tradition of the importance of self-presentation to outsiders and knowledge sharing within the group that subsequently moved into published sources as hoboes faded from the American scene and men like Charlie sought to preserve their memories of that important aspect of American life.

The only elements usually found in hobo autobiographies but missing from Charlie's *Tales* is extensive reference to why he started on the road and why he left it. The reason for this difference is key.

Most of the earlier autobiographies fall into four main categories. In one group, the hobo experience is regarded as a temporary, generally romantic interlude in the author's life. This can take different forms depending on the personality and class of the writer. In the case of an upper-class Englishman like George Witten, whose family tree traces back to A.D. 800, it is an introduction to the adventurous life and a way for him to connect with the brigand ancestor with whom he identifies, and it finally leads him back into his class to serve the Empire in the Boer War. "Then I had my first thrilling sensation of being an outlaw. When I was pulled through the door of the box-car I was pulled into another world, a world of adventure and hardship. . . . I had stepped outside the laws into a realm where men lived by their wits. If we were caught it meant prison, but the idea filled me with an elation hard to describe."[3] Since hoboing is only a passing stage, little attention is given to it for its own sake, and most of Witten's description focuses on Africa.

For more middle-class youth hoboing is also a temporary interlude, but it is usually linked more to a transition stage in the life-cycle than to the psychological dynamics of finding one's place within a family heritage. Consequently, at the end of the autobiography the author returns to the same "real life" he would have originally assumed without time on the road. One example of this is John Peele, who writes about the hobo trip he made throughout Arizona and New Mexico. He began his journey West after graduating from Massey Business College in Richmond, Virginia, seeking to improve his asthma. He wrote his autobiography not to record hobo life but in the hope that the "book demonstrates the value of physical culture and education to the American youth as the author believes no other work upon the market has yet done."[4]

The classic example of this type of hobo autobiography is Glen Mullin's *Adventures of a Scholar Tramp* (1925).[5] Mullin begins his autobiography as he waits in Chicago's Englewood Station to hop his first train. The autobiography follows Mullin on his transition from a "gay-cat" (newcomer) to a seasoned hobo through his initiation into the same formative experiences Charlie recounts—learning to ride different sorts of trains, begging, and being arrested and jailed. Throughout Mullin's book, however, the reader is left wondering why he is a *scholar* tramp. Certainly the book is replete with Latinate words, classical allusions, and transcendentalist reveries on nature, but why? Only in the closing chapter does Mullin reveal that he is spending the summer between college and art school riding the rails. He does not need to reveal anything about his previous life or discuss why he leaves the road, because the road is not "real," it is just an adventure that existed apart from and had no impact on his personality or life course.

A second kind of autobiography uses the author's past to help sensationalize his life on the road. In these autobiographies the author describes the conventional nature of his early life and his respectability after leaving the road in order to present his life on the road as an initiation into a strange (and nostalgically wonderful) way of life which demonstrates his strength, toughness, and ability to mingle with the underworld. The best example of this tendency is

Josiah Flynt Willard's *My Life* (1908), which established his reputation for hobnobbing with criminals and his ability to get along on the road.[6] He associated the road and the criminals he met there with self-expression, assertion, and freedom; the road was where he lost his shyness, his lack of direction, and his inability to participate, which he felt in the respectable world with its strictures of Methodist morality, the WCTU, and his famous aunt Francis Willard. On the road Flynt virtually created himself as a character. Though the road met Flynt's needs, he felt no loyalty to it and returned from a European trip to work as a railroad policeman. Flynt restricts his portrait of the road to the criminal elements (which Charlie readily confirms as there) but fails to portray the vast majority of men who are harvest hands, mule skinners, carpenters, or simply unemployed laborers—their presence doesn't fit into his psychological needs, and a true picture of the world of the road is not his foremost intention.

A third category of autobiography is distinguished by gender. When women like Bertha Thompson or Barbara Starke write about hoboing, they have to do so as marginal members of the group.[7] They are clearly outside the proper social roles for women, but they do not really fit into the male-oriented world of hoboes either. As women they are forced to create their own community of outsiders at the edge of the hoboes' world.

In the fourth category of hobo autobiography, life on the road is an experience that changes the individual's life and makes growth beyond the prescribed limits of class possible. One variation of this formula of hobo life for working-class youth is political. Hoboing assumes importance primarily as the setting which introduces the rider to radical politics. When I interviewed Fred Thompson, the official historian of the IWW, he spoke of his hobo experiences at first only in passing—he thought of himself so much as a Wobbly that an identity as a hobo did not immediately surface.[8] A literary example of the same phenomenon is

Charles Ashleigh's *Rambling Kid*, which chronicles "Joe Crane's" road experience as a necessary transition in his transformation from farm kid, to IWW activist, to American expatriot propagandist for the Bolshevik revolution.[9]

Another variant is more intellectual. For Nels Anderson, author of the famous 1926 sociological study *The Hobo*, life on the road gave him not only the opportunity to leave home and eventually pursue higher education but also the expertise which ultimately launched (and paradoxically limited) his career as a sociologist, a process detailed in his 1975 autobiography *The American Hobo*.[10] For others, hoboing launched their careers as writers. Though Charlie dislikes Jim Tully, it remains true that the road gave Tully his self-education and his start as a writer.[11]

The most famous writer in the group, Jack London, embodies both transformations. *The Road*, originally written as a series of essays for *Cosmopolitan Magazine* in 1907, chronicles his travels with Kelly's Army (the western branch of Coxey's Army) in 1894 and his other hobo travels.[12] These autobiographical recollections primarily serve to reveal London as knowledgeable about the ways of the road yet good-hearted, and they do so in such a way that the more he exhibits knowledge of socially unacceptable behavior the more his innate nobility triumphs and the followers of conventional morality appear priggish and preposterous. Though *The Road* leaves the political dimension of the experience unstated, London clearly states in his essays "How I Became a Socialist" and "What Life Means to Me" that his hobo experiences both changed his politics from individualist to socialist and convinced him that his future lay in working with his brain, not with his back, thereby leading to his literary career.[13]

And how does Charlie Fox fit into this neat, academic typology? In an important sense, he doesn't. One of the things that increasingly strikes me as important about Charlie's *Tales* is that he never uses the wanderlust as an escape from things in his life. There is no sense that something

outside himself is "making" him do things or that he is using psychological or sociological conditions to justify his life.
Charlie plays the hand that life deals him—sometimes good,
sometimes bad—and just tries to do the best he can with
the cards he has. There is a true sense of honor and respect
for the values of working-class culture shining through this
book. This sense is very different from what I find in many of
the other autobiographies such as Flynt's, John Worby's, or
Charles Barth's.[14] In their works the wanderlust is a way of
naming and justifying avoidance of anything they find difficult to handle. Perhaps in part the difference is because
Charlie's story doesn't refer to things outside itself. Charlie's
hoboing just *is*—part of life, not what he uses to avoid
something else or move into something else, or something
he needs to justify. Perhaps for this reason it is one of the
purest chronicles of hobo life ever written, though written
about a time after the great heyday of the hoboes. Nevertheless, the lure of the road was still strong enough to attract
Charlie and hold him for ten years.

Charlie and those like him who took to the road in the
1920s and remained there through the Great Depression
are not the same as those desperate train-hoppers of the
1930s who moved in an often hopeless search for some job,
somewhere. As Charlie remarks, "We spent a lot of time
keeping them fellas out of trouble." It is a mark of how completely we have lost sight of the real hoboes that so many
Americans regard the 1930s as the heyday of the hobo. It is
my belief that Charlie Fox's *Tales of an American Hobo* can
do much to restore this group to its rightful place in our
history.

LYNNE M. ADRIAN

Notes

Note: The research on hobo autobiographies was supported
in part by an award from the University of Alabama Research Grants Committee.

1. Ben L. Reitman Papers, University of Illinois–Chicago Circle Campus.

2. *Hobo News*, later retitled *Hobo World*, Cincinnati, Ohio. The two monthly newspapers appear to have been different titles for one continuous publication running from 1913 until at least 1930. Few issues of the newspaper remain, making exact dates difficult to obtain.

3. George Witten, *Outlaw Trails: A Yankee Hobo Soldier of the Queen* (New York: Minton, Balch and Company, 1929), p. 9.

4. John Peele, *From North Carolina to Southern California without a Ticket* (Tarboro, N.C.: Edwards and Broughton Printing Company, 1907), p. 6.

5. Glen Hawthorne Mullin, *Adventures of a Scholar Tramp* (New York: Century, 1925).

6. Josiah Flynt Willard, *Tramping with Tramps: Studies and Sketches of Vagabond Life* (New York: Century Company, 1899).

7. Ben Lewis Reitman, *Sister of the Road: The Autobiography of Box-Car Bertha as Told to Dr. Ben L. Reitman* (New York: Macaulay Company, 1937; repr. New York: Harper Colophon, 1975, Amok Press, 1988); Barbara Starke (pseud.), *Born in Captivity. The Story of a Girl's Escape* (Indianapolis, Ind.: Bobbs-Merrill, 1931).

8. Fred Thompson, personal interview, March 1979.

9. Charles Ashleigh, *Rambling Kid* (London: Faber, 1930).

10. Nels Anderson, *The Hobo: The Sociology of the Homeless Man. A Study Prepared for the Chicago Council of Social Agencies under the Direction of the Committee on Homeless Men* (Chicago: University of Chicago Press, 1923); and *The American Hobo: An Autobiography* (Leiden: Brill, 1975).

11. Jim Tully, *Beggars of Life: A Hobo Autobiography* (New York: Albert and Charles Boni, 1924).

12. Jack London, *The Road* (New York: Macmillan, 1907).

13. Richard W. Etulain (ed.), *Jack London on the Road: The Tramp Diary and Other Hobo Writings* (Logan: Utah State University Press, 1979).

14. John Worby, *The Other Half: The Autobiography of a Tramp* (New York: Lee Furman, 1937); Charles P. Barth, *Hobo Trail to Nowhere* (Philadelphia: Whitmore Publishing Company, 1969).

TALES OF AN AMERICAN HOBO

HOBOES

The origin or specific meaning of the word *hobo* is unknown. There are several theories that have been put forth over the years, but there is no concrete proof that any of them is the absolute truth. The only thing that we know for a fact is that the term *hobo* came into being shortly after the Civil War, as did the first train hoppers also show up in this same time frame. Hopping trains soon became synonymous with the term *hobo*.

There are distinct differences between hoboes, tramps, and bums which due to the limited knowledge and experience of the average person are unknown.

I was born and partly raised on a farm and was taught to believe that hoboes, tramps and bums were one and the same thing. Nothing could be farther from the truth.

The hobo was a wanderer and homeless vagabond who rode trains whenever possible. The hobo was the forerunner of the migratory workers. The hobo would take most any available work in order to pay his way. The hobo was largely averse to panhandling or mooching and would always offer to work for whatever he was forced to mooch when he was broke.

If a hobo got a steady job that he liked and he was getting along with his boss and the management in general, he would often work steady for two or three years before the "rambling fever" got the best of him. Many of these men were skilled workers and trustworthy and conscientious employees. It was quite common for an employer to hire the same man fifteen or twenty times over a period of twenty or twenty-five years.

The hobo was essentially a wanderer. A free spirited human, who put his personal freedom ahead of his desire for worldly gain. He was neither greedy nor competitive. Nor did his philosophy detract from his character in any sense. Of course, there were bad hoboes, just as there are bad people in all walks of life. A bad hobo usually had a bad time wherever he went, for the average hobo had nothing but contempt for anyone he couldn't trust. Hoboes had what was called the code of the road and also had what was known as the rule of the jungle. Many hobo jungle camps wouldn't allow a drunk to light there, and dope fiends and troublemakers of any kind usually got beaten up and ejected bodily as soon as they were found out. They used to say, "Junkies have no place in the jungle." This jungle rule was good, for it contributed to better, more respectable living.

Hobo discipline was inflexible. There were no appeals and no plea bargaining in the jungle. The true tramp didn't ride trains. They walked the highways and byways. They were less prone to work for what they got than was a true hobo. They usually had some kind of a gimmick such as peddling lead pencils, thread, buttons, soap, shoe strings, and so on from house to house.

I have seen tramp palm readers, fortune-tellers and tramp preachers who would preach you a one-hour sermon for a meal and fifty cents. Those dudes looked the part and knew the Bible by heart. All of them carried a Bible under their arm or in their hand wherever they went.

The bum is quite another story, for the true bum is usually a town drunk who seldom if ever gets outside his hometown during his lifetime.

They are usually found on streets and street corners mooching nickels and dimes from passersby or hanging around some cheap tavern mooching drinks from overly drunk or overly generous customers. These bums always have a sad story to tell, and many of them will even cry real tears while they are telling you about their mother dying with a heart attack, or their beloved wife of twenty-nine beautiful years, dying last week with cancer. If you aren't careful you will be crying with them or taking a mortgage on your home so you can loan this poor unhappy man a few

2

bucks in his hour of need. So as the all-time King of the Hoboes Jeff Davis used to say, "Hoboes will work. Tramps won't and bums can't." A few tramps did work.

The question has often been asked, Why would anyone choose to become a hobo, tramp, or bum? The reasons are countless. Chief among them is child abuse or any unsatisfactory conditions or situations in the home that a child might deem intolerable. Secondly is the death of a loved one, and the list goes on and on.

There were quite a few escaped convicts and fugitives from county jails and state penal farms, chain gangs, road gang work camps, and so on. There were also a lot of jack-rollers (muggers), dips (pickpockets), second-story men (burglars), and a goodly percentage of genuine professional yeggs (hoodlums) known as Pete men (safe blowers) and heisters (stickup men) and all manner of petty thieves, referred to as hand-burglars.

These people used to infiltrate the hobo jungles and mingle with the hoboes to some extent, purely for the purpose of anonymity. They were using the hoboes as a shield, to safeguard their true identity if the "bulls" should show up, but there was never any true comradeship between the true hoboes and the hoodlum element of jungle society. The two groups had nothing in common and managed to survive together by an unwritten law, to wit: "You leave me alone and I won't bother you." So the true hoboes and the hoodlum riffraff of the hobo jungles survived together under conditions that were essentially an armed truce at best.

As in all segments of society, some hoboes were inclined to become a little egotistical in their later life. It is common knowledge that the true professional hobo was the upper crust of the vagabond battalions. Some seemed to forget that about 98 percent of all hoboes got their start as tramps or bums.

I never met a hobo that hadn't walked the highways at various times as a common tramp. Nor have I ever seen one that hadn't been forced to beg, bum, mooch, ding, and panhandle when he was broke and hungry. Some were even forced to steal food. The professional hobo was a survival expert, but even so there were times when circumstances would force him back into the amateur ranks temporarily, where you had to rely on a catch-as-catch-can existence until you could score for two or three days work and get back in the chips.

In the 1920s there were estimated to be about one hundred thousand hoboes in the United States. These figures related to the train-riding, homeless migratory workers only.

To my knowledge, there was never even an effort made to estimate the approximate number of tramps on the road at any given time. During the Depression years, which ran from October 1929 to December 1941, there were millions of homeless, jobless people wandering around the country and millions more who were afraid or averse to leaving their hometowns. They stood in long soup lines or any kind of lines for hours, seven days a week, to get a handout. There were thousands of rescue missions all over the country with soup kitchens, and many of them had free flophouses where people could sleep in bad weather or any kind of weather if they were unwilling to sleep on the ground in a park or wherever they could find a place to lie down. It was estimated that there were somewhere between one million and two and a half million train hoppers, not true hoboes, on the railroads during the worst part of the depression. These were just common home guards, including factory workers, college graduates, professional people of all kinds, ranchers, farmers, and business people of all kinds. Many of them fell off trains or under trains, due to a lack of experience, and many were murdered by jack-rollers, who mistakenly assumed that certain ones of these train hoppers had money.

Unfortunately, these people were all victims of the times. As an example: Consider the list of names of hoboes who later became famous and known at least nationwide. To mention a few, I will list Clark Gable, Groucho Marx, Art Linkletter, Eric Sevareid, William O. Douglas, chief justice of the U.S. Supreme Court, also Woody Guthrie, Jimmie Rogers of Nashville fame, and so on. Earlier hoboes that made it big included Wm. Harrison (Jack Dempsey), Jack London, Jim Tully, and many others and let's not leave Winthrop Rockefeller out.

Contrary to popular belief, hoboes were not a typed species of humanity. Some of the modern old-time hoboes want to give the impression that hoboes were a distinct type of humanity. This is not true, for the worn-out shoes, patched pants, and shapeless torn hat was purely the figment of some newspaper artist's imagination shortly after the Civil War. This impression is purely a caricature of what the average hobo looked like and not a factual description.

The true hobo tried to keep himself as clean and as well dressed as he could under the circumstances. Two of the oldest professional practicing hoboes living today are "Frisco Jack" Sopko and John "Fry Pan Jack" Fisk. These men are good examples of what I am talking about.

I have known Frisco and Fry Pan for over fifty years and I have never seen either of them when they could have been considered as unkempt and slovenly.

There were legions of quite respectable hoboes, of which I knew quite a few of the best. Most if not all the following named men are dead, but I am proud to say that most of them were personal friends of mine. "Powder River Slim" Caldwell, "Smokey Joe" Evans, "Soldier" Fields, "Battling Jack" Ross, Mongo "Neck Bones Shorty" Penman, Wayne "Dido George" Brannon, "Flannel Mouth Shorty" Shannon, "Shorty" Harris, Wade "Yellow Hair" Palmer, Knute "The Cook" Hofius, Ray "Alabam" Green, "Chicken Red" Donvan, Pat "Bacon Butts" Kincaid, Elmer "Big Stony" Stone, "Blackie" Renfro, Jeff Davis, Woodie Guthrie, "Ducky" Mead, "Cooge" Wiggins, "Slim" Meadows, "Tex" Murray, "Minneapolis Red" Johnson, "Sioux City" Charlie Drake, and a host of others.

These men could walk down any street in any town and not attract any undue or unfavorable attention, and this virtue belongs to the old-time professional hobo.

No true hobo wanted to be so unique that he would attract the attention of the town bulls, wherever he went.

In the heyday of the true hoboes, you could usually tell what section of the country a "bo" was from by what he was carrying or wasn't carrying. The bos in the western half of the country nearly all carried bedrolls or blanket rolls, whereas the eastern bos rarely if ever carried a bedroll.

The New York bos usually carried two things, a safety razor and a daily newspaper (the *New York Times*) if they could get hold of a copy. They would read the stock market report off and on all day, then use the paper for a blanket at night if the weather was cool or cold. If the weather was hot they would spread the paper on the ground at night and use it for a bed.

I have never been able to figure out why a bo would be concerned with the stock market report.

I used to get four or five dollars ahead now and then and go to some Goodwill Industries Store and dress up like the duke of Macaroni. I used to get nearly new Florsheim dress slippers for a dollar to a dollar seventy-five a pair. Good socks for five to ten cents a pair. Good dress pants and shirts for fifteen to twenty cents each. Once I got an almost new Hart-Schaffner and Marx sport top coat for eighty-five cents. This was a forty-five-dollar coat and it was like new.

Contrary to some modern writings I have read, there was very little glamour and romance in the life of a hobo. This was a hard, dangerous, and often very lonely life.

About the only social life a hobo had or could actually expect would be in a hobo jungle, where he might meet a friend or friends or make a new friend or two and spend two or three days around a campfire exchanging tales of the road, cooking stew, and drinking gallons of black coffee. The only real assets a hobo had was a reasonable freedom from responsibility and the great value and importance of his true friends.

Nearly every hobo had anywhere from a few to many friends scattered all over the country, people (home guards) that had never been anyplace nor saw very many, if any, hard days. These people have never missed a meal and never had to sleep on the ground or on park benches and in straw stacks, railroad sand houses, and even jails in bitterly cold weather. Yet these were the people who seemed to see a lot of romance in the life of hoboes. They usually looked upon their hobo friends as heroes of some sort.

As "Steam Train Maury" Graham has so often said, "Friends are the sum total of a hobo's wealth."

Who would be more qualified to make such a statement than a five times king of all the hoboes east of the Mississippi River by decree?

Anything that a human has anything to do with must of necessity be a conglomeration of good and bad. So it was that there were both good and bad hobo jungles all over the United States in the heyday of the hoboes.

A good jungle was a peaceful, systematically run home for vagabonds, whereas a bad jungle was a miserable hellhole, virtually unfit for human habitation.

These bad jungles harbored troublemakers, jungle thieves, and degenerates of all kinds. This was an ideal environment for the likes of the hobo writer Jim Tully, who was so depraved that his motto was "Women for breeding purposes and young boys for pleasure."

Even at this late date I will affirm that I and fifty thousand other bos would have welcomed the chance to kill Mr. Tully.

Contrary to the teachings and assertions of ignorant people, about 95 percent of all true hoboes could not be considered as depraved in any sense.

The Hobo's Oath will confirm this statement. Quote: I Joe Dokes or any name solemnly swear to do all in my power to aid and assist all those willing to aid and assist themselves.

7

I pledge myself to assist all runaway boys and girls and induce them to return to their homes and parents. I solemnly swear never to take advantage of my fellow men or be unjust to others, and to do all in my power for the betterment of myself, my organization, and America. So help me God. Signed, Joe Dokes or whatever.

Since the true hobo is rapidly becoming a thing of the past, I thought it expedient that I write a little book on the life of a hobo, his true experiences as he lived them, and the ups and downs in the everyday life of the knights of the road.

This pseudo-title was dreamed up perhaps by some writer or movie producer back in the 1930s, for it was at that time that I heard that some author had written a book called *Knights of the Road*, and later I heard that they had produced a movie by the same name.

Being one of these "knights" in reality, I didn't have the money to buy a copy of the book nor the fifteen or twenty cents to go see the movie.

Regardless of my financial status or who coined the title, I am grateful to the creator of the title in the context that it tends to put a little glamour into a profession that was always very unglamorous from the standpoint of conventional society. Most people never really knew a genuine hobo and most of them didn't want to. Those that had the common decency to talk to a hobo, as one human to another, usually found them to be pretty interesting people. Many times I have heard some kid holler at his mother, "Mommy, here comes some old tramp to the door." Then Mommy usually came to the door and told you that she had fed four or five men already today and she didn't have anything to give to you.

If she was a kind-hearted person she would fix you a couple of sandwiches of cold soup beans or cold fried potatoes, wrap them up, and hand them out the door to you. Those soup bean and potato sandwiches are fine eating when you are hungry.

One thing I learned before I had been on the road long was, never ask a wealthy or even a high-toned middle-class person for anything if you expect to eat or get whatever you are asking for. The poor people will usually go out of their way to be nice to you if you are nice to them. A Catholic priest was usually good for the price of a meal or a flop (a bed) if the weather was too bad to stay outside. The large majority of Protestant ministers wouldn't give a hobo the time of day. A Methodist preacher in Denver, Colorado, became very indignant and threatened to put me in jail for asking if he could spare ten or fifteen cents for me to get something to eat.

The Salvation Army was the old standby in an emergency, and they seldom gave you any trouble. I always offered to work for my meal or bed and that seemed to please them and they would even invite me to come back if I ever needed a favor when I happened to be in that town again. I only got "clipped" at one Sally (Salvation Army) and that was in Laramie, Wyoming. Some old Scotsman who was in charge of the kitchen, free meals, and beds had me split a cord and one-half of wood and had my buddy shovel two tons of coal through a window down into the basement for our breakfast.

When we finished he called us into the dining room and gave us each two thin pancakes and some weak sugar molasses and a glass of blue-John (skimmed milk). No coffee, a guy would really have to be weird that would drink skimmed milk for breakfast instead of coffee. Needless to say, old Scotty made believers out of us, for we never again stopped at the Laramie Sally.

BECOMING A HOBO

My initiation into life on the road wasn't any different from countless thousands of other "road kids" before and since. When I reached the point where life became unbearable at home, I took off down the road with no definite purpose nor destination in mind.

On May 25, 1928 I made up a small pack by rolling my clothes in two old army blankets and I was ready to hit the road. I had no idea of how to survive without a job or without a few dollars to guarantee my survival.

I hitchhiked the ten miles into Terre Haute and headed east on the old national road, U.S. 40. U.S. 40 highway was a gravel road in those days. I started thumbing all the eastbound cars and by late afternoon I was in Indianapolis. Having covered a total of eighty-two miles.

I went out on New York Street to visit an aunt and uncle of mine, where I could get a meal and most likely a good bed to sleep in that night. At the breakfast table the next morning, my uncle told me that I could get a job at the Stutz automobile plant. I got a job as a roustabout for at age fifteen I wasn't qualified for a skill of any kind. I worked there until late September, then hitchhiked to Kokomo, and on October 4, 1928 I got a job at the D. C. Jenkins Glass Company and worked there until February 1929 and hitchhiked back to Indianapolis and got a job at Kingans Packing Company in the sausage department as a meat stamper. I was doing OK until March 15 when I met a professional hobo by the name of "Flannel Mouth Shorty" Shannon.

His tales of the road fascinated me and I began to give some thought to becoming a hobo and told Shorty how I felt. He said, "Well, kid, if you really want to hit the road, meet me in front of the Gem Theater at noon on Saturday,

March 17, 1929. Roll your belongings up in your blankets and we will grab us a freight train."

Up to this point, I had never even thought of riding a freight train, for I had been told they were the most dangerous thing on earth. I was very nervous and afraid to tackle that first one. But Shorty explained the techniques in detail and I lost some of my fear.

We walked down Morris Street to where the Belt Line came aground the south edge of the city and intersected with the main lines of the New York Central (Big 4) and the Pennsylvania. Before long we grabbed a Big 4 freight as she went on the main and a whole new life was begun.

The next morning we were at 6th and Broadway in St. Louis, which was at that time the headquarters of St. Louis skid row. Those slums didn't appeal to me, so we walked out North Broadway to the Wabash Railroad yards and caught a freight train to Kansas City.

Three days later we was in Denver, Colorado. We walked south of Denver down the Denver and Rio Grand Western Railroad three or four miles and tried to domesticate a half-grown cub bear and Shorty came out second best, so we gave up on the wild bears. We headed back East and wound up in Louisville, Kentucky. Shorty went to see a friend while I went to a show. The next day he went his way and I went mine. I imagine old Shorty is long dead. Most of the old ones are gone. The rest of *Tales of an American Hobo* is just a lot of memories of my life as a hobo.

It is not the history of a good easy life, but it is the true events of the life of an American farm boy turned hobo.

THE DENVER SUIT

I hit Denver one time and I was almost barefooted and the seat and knees were out of my pants, so I knew I was going to have to promote some shoes and clothing, and do it fast. I stopped at the first funeral parlor I came to and put "the B" on the undertaker, and lo and behold he said, "Come back here, I think I have just what you need." We went into a back room and I saw a new suit and new shoes and a hat lying on a table. He explained to me that a holdup man was killed yesterday and he was just about your size. He picked up the vest and showed me the bullet hole in it and the blood-stained lining, then threw the vest into the incinerator. He told me to try the suit, shoes, and hat on. They fit like they were made for me. Let me tell you, friend, it isn't often you get a tailor-made Hart-Schaffner and Marx suit, Stacy Adams shoes, and a Stetson hat for free.

When I thanked him and walked out of there I was really decked out, or so I felt.

I almost ruined that new outfit the very next day, out in the northeast end of Denver, in the Rock Island yards. I was waiting for a train to come out, heading for Chicago. Me and another guy was sitting on a rail smoking and talking when I happened to look toward the west end of the yards and what I saw almost caused my heart to stop. There were fifty or seventy-five cops coming right at us on a dead run.

I told the other guy, "Get down in that ditch and bend down and run down under that viaduct and up the bank on the other side onto that highway and we will walk right out in the country and they can't come after us." This is what we did and we made a clean getaway, but some places along that ditch was wet and muddy and I got mud all over my new shoes and pant cuffs.

We were in Greeley, Colorado, that evening and when the paper came out a big headline read: "Denver Police Round Up 155 Hoboes in Rock Island Yards." This was in August 1932.

HITTING THE COW AT LEBEC

When I was coming back from the West Coast I had gotten into the habit of catching a train out of Sacramento, on the U.P. over "the hump," and down into Reno and Sparks, Nevada, then east on to Cheyenne, Wyoming, then catch the D.&R.G.W. (Denver and Rio Grande Western) out of Cheyenne down to Denver, then catch a Rock Island (redball) to Chicago and catch a C.&E.I. rattler (freight train) to Terre Haute, my hometown.

The hump I spoke of is the high Sierra Nevada mountains east of Sacramento, California, known as Donner Pass.

I came out of Los Angeles one time, hitchhiking up the north main street or San Fernando road until it intersected with the Ridge Route, U.S. 1 or the Pacific highway, and went on into Bakersfield. I got a ride with some rancher down there around Saugus or Castiac and he hauled me almost to Lebec, a little town on the western slope about ten thousand feet above and forty miles uphill from Bakersfield.

This guy turned off the highway into a canyon and stopped. He said, "This is where you get out, buddy."

I thanked him and unloaded, then I realized how dark it was. I started walking toward the lights of Lebec, which were about two miles below me. It was so dark you couldn't see your hand if you held it right in front of your face, and you couldn't tell where the road was only by feel. If you walked off the pavement into that loose shale shoulder you knew it was time to turn one way or the other and get back on the road or risk falling a thousand feet straight down.

I was groping my way through that total darkness when all of a sudden I ran into something alive that let out a fearful roar. Not knowing what it was I hit it five or six times before either of us could move, then I jumped back and jerked my pocketknife out, opened it, and got ready for business. I could still hear some noise, but whatever it was didn't attack me. So I took out a box of safety matches and struck one, and there in front of me stood eight big red and white steers. I walked around them by match light and went on down the road. I finally got to Lebec and I was never so glad to see a town in my life.

I went into an all-night restaurant and mooched the proprietor for a hamburger and a cup of coffee. He said, "Well, I guess I can spare you that much." Some guy sitting there at the counter said, "Come here, buddy, and order up whatever you want and I'll pay for it."

We ate and talked and when we got through he asked me what kind of cigarettes I smoked? I told him, "When I smoke hard rolls I seem to like Luckies best." He got me two packs of Luckies and told me, "You are welcome to ride on into Bakersfield with me if you want to."

As dark as it was up there in those mountains I would have been glad to ride a wild bear if he was going to Bakersfield.

On the way down he mentioned that he was originally from Terre Haute, Indiana, and it turned out that I knew his dad, a Mr. Fred Watts, who had been Vigo County truant officer during my school days. Mr. Watts had been all set to send me to the Indiana Boys School when I was in the seventh grade for hitting a schoolteacher in the jaw with one of those big old gray arithmetic books. When he found out the truth about the matter he apologized to me and put the teacher on probation, permanently. When I mentioned this, I was amazed to hear this man say, "I've heard Dad talk about that case many times. He always said that you wasn't a bad boy, that the teacher simply goaded you into becoming violent."

When we got to Bakersfield he gave me eight dollars and invited me to go home with him and spend the rest of the night, but I declined and thanked him for everything and went out to the edge of town and crawled in behind a big Richlube sign and got a few hours of much-needed sleep.

KLAMATH INDIANS
AT THE DAM

It was on this same trip that I visited Klamath Falls, Oregon, for the first time, and what a visit it turned out to be. The town sits along the banks of the Klamath River at the falls. That is where the town got its name. As usual I headed for the river to look around, for since all this sight-seeing was free, I didn't intend to miss any of it. There was a suspension foot bridge that was suspended on steel cables right over the top of the falls. There were several Indian men and boys out on the bridge engaged in spearing salmon. The men would spear them as they came up over the falls and the boys would put them in gunnysacks and carry them up on top of a low hill to where the women and big girls were dressing and smoking the fish for future use.

I was raised along the Wabash River and had taken fish all different ways but this was a new experience for me. It took a lot of speed and accuracy to spear those fish while they were jumping up over the falls in that swift water.

I got to talking with the two men nearest to me and one asked me if I was hungry? I said, "Yes." He told his son to take me up on the hill and have your mother give him some smoked fish. We went up there and he spoke to her in Indian and gave her his dad's message. She smiled and spoke, then picked up a large butcher knife and cut off a chunk of fish that I am sure must have weighed one and a half or two pounds and handed it to me and invited me to sit on a chair and rest while I was eating. I thanked her and sat down and started eating. She asked me if I was on the road? I said, "Yes." Then she began to talk about what a terrible shape the country was in, and about the thousands of people who came through Klamath Falls every year. She said, "You know, this Depression makes me wonder whether or not the white man's way really is best, as they have always claimed." I told her that in my opinion no one's way is any good unless it will provide for the needs of the people and give them a reasonable amount of security.

When I finally finished eating my fish, she grabbed that knife and started to cut me another hunk and I had a hard time convincing her that I couldn't possibly eat any more right now. There is a funny side to this story that occurred to me when I was eating that smoked fish.

My dad's father was half Delaware Indian and French and half Pennsylvania Dutch and he used to smoke enough fish every summer to last all through the winter at least. He smoked carp, buffalo, and red horse and stored them in wooden boxes.

I had to grin to myself when I thought of how I used to hate to eat smoked fish when I was a kid. But here I was eating smoked salmon and thinking how good it tasted. If Grandpa was looking down at me now, what was he thinking? He used to cut off a chunk of smoked fish with his hunting knife and he had to force me to eat it.

It is amazing how time, conditions, and circumstances can alter the pattern of your life and even your thinking processes. After a few hours' visit, I bade these kind people farewell, but they wouldn't let me leave until I accepted a big chunk of salmon that she had put in a paper bag for me to have with me, just in case I got hungry.

THE JEWS
IN THE ROADSIDE PARK

Between walking and hitchhiking I was a good ways north of Klamath Falls by the next afternoon, when I came to a nice park on the east side of the road, so I decided to go over under one of those big trees and lie down and rest for two or three hours. As I entered the park I saw a group of men, women, and children some distance from me and by the way it looked I assumed they were Jews and were celebrating some sort of a Jewish holiday. They said, "We have plenty of food and if you are hungry you are welcome to eat, if you like Jewish food."

They didn't need to make any excuses nor apologies, for I never saw a tramp that accepted or rejected food on the basis of its ethnic qualities.

I joined them at the tables and was apparently accepted as a kindred soul, for they all seemed to feel that they couldn't do enough for me. They just kept shoving food at me and as a result I ate until I was in misery. All this time they were busy trying to get me to tell them all about the life of a hobo and where I had been and the things I had seen.

I ate so many pickled herrings that I was afraid a wild cat might come out of the surrounding woods and eat me, thinking I was a fish.

I tried to excuse myself and go back to my shade tree so they could continue their celebration, but they wouldn't hear to such a thing. They wanted me to talk about my way of life, so I did until it was almost sundown.

The women filled a pasteboard box full of food for me so I could be assured of eating for a day or two. When they were ready to leave I had to shake hands with all of them, including the kids.

18

There was water there in the park and I had food so I camped there for a couple of days and just took it easy.

In some respects it was really nice back in those days, for no one seemed to care where you camped or jungled up so long as you didn't destroy something, steal, or start a forest fire or something of that nature. In the past twenty-five years or so you can't do much of anything without getting someone's permission, and the average permit of any kind costs you x number of dollars and must be issued according to some code, zoning law, or commission that has full authority to grant or deny anything. For the benefit of everyone concerned, we had better elect some people to the Congress and Senate that will vote down and out all this type of foolishness before we find ourselves right in the middle of a big Communist dictatorship and a rebellion. We don't need anyone to tell us how to live and what we can do, and to add insult to injury, charge us for doing it. I will always respect and obey the bona fide laws of the land, but the bureaucratic laws, edicts, and mandates are purely a mercenary gimmick used to put unfair pressures and restrictions on the American people in general, and as such are in nowise to be considered as bona fide and just laws in any sense.

During my years on the road I visited many national parks and scenic spots all over the country and seldom did anyone ever ask me what I was doing there. Not once did anyone ask, "Who gave you permission to be here?"

Yes, we need to reestablish the true concept of a free America as we used to know it. We can only do this by getting rid of the bureaucrats and let them get out and work for a living just the same as about 85 percent of the Americans do. The 15 percent have always been the idle rich, the afflicted, the women and children, and the hoboes, and even a hobo does at least some honest work.

SWIMMING IN THE OCEAN
IN OREGON

When I left Pickled Herring Park I walked along up the highway until I came to a place where the highway ran parallel to the ocean for two or three miles, and you could look right down on the beach and hear the breakers slapping against the big rocks that lay in a broken line in the shallow water along the edge of the beach.

I saw several people down there bathing and splashing around in the surf so I decided to join them and soak awhile and get cooled off and get a bath at the same time. I had an old pair of bathing trunks that I had found so I ducked in behind a big rock and changed clothes, then I walked along the beach to where the swimmers were. I introduced myself and as I was standing there in water about hip deep talking to one of the men, a heavy breaker came in and slammed me up against a big rock and came pretty close to skinning me up but good. I barely managed to get my hands up and catch myself before my face hit that rock. I stayed there an hour or two and went on my way.

END OF STEEL
AT PRINCE GEORGE

I went on up through Oregon and Washington and crossed the sound at Bellingham on a ferry. A man from Vancouver, British Columbia, picked me up in a pickup truck and we started on north. I asked him about me crossing the Canadian border. He said, "Don't worry about that, I will tell him you are my nephew and that you are going home with me for two or three weeks."

He told them this story and they let us cross, perhaps because they knew this man.

When I got to Vancouver I decided to ride trains from here on, as I was planning to go to Alaska and I didn't want to do any walking or spend any nights in those mountains, with the bears and all those other wild creatures. I was never too brave when you get right down to the hard facts. I caught a train that was mostly flatcars like they haul logs on, so I just sat there and enjoyed the scenery, and what scenery it is! British Columbia is undoubtedly one of the most beautiful places in the world. We finally came to a town where the train went in on a siding (switch track) and the engineer uncoupled the engine and went down the track a short distance to a turntable and turned the engine around and headed south to the south switch and backed in on the siding and hooked on to the caboose.

I ran down there and asked the brakeman what they were going to do? He said, "After we get something to eat we are going back to Vancouver."

I asked, "When will there be a train going on to Alaska?"

He said, "I don't know, this is the end of steel, so it might be a long time before they get the steel laid on up there." Then he laughed and said, "If you don't mind walking it is

21

only about a thousand miles right straight north through those mountains and woods."

I had all I wanted of that, so I asked, "How about riding back to Vancouver with you?"

He said, "You will have to talk to the conductor, but I'm sure it will be all right."

I asked the conductor and he rather grudgingly said, "Yeah, I guess you can ride back, but you will have to ride on the back porch of the caboose."

This I gladly agreed to, for I wanted to get back into a country where the high steel went somewhere, anywhere. Time has dimmed my memory but I think this end-of-steel town was either Prince George or Fort George.

STEALING THE BURRITOS
AT MIDWAY

Once when I was crossing the Great Salt Lake the train stopped at Midway Island, which was a man-made island where there were a few camp cars parked on a siding and a Mexican section crew that lived there for the sole purpose of maintaining that thirty-mile bridge where the U.P. (Union Pacific) crossed the lake. The car I was on stopped right alongside of the kitchen and dining car and through an open window in the kitchen end I could see a large pile of burritos stacked on a table right by the window. I climbed down and went into the kitchen and put the B on the cook. He refused to give me anything. I was hungry so I decided there must be a way, and I remembered what my dad used to say, "Where there is a will, there's always a way." There were three or four big rough Pennsylvania Dutch boys on the train with me, so I picked out two of them and asked, "Do you guys want to eat?"

They said, "Yes." I said, "OK, go up to the other end of the dining car and start a fake fight and keep cursing, swinging and kicking until the train starts to move out, then climb aboard and I'll have enough food for all of us."

When the fight started all the Mexicans ran up there to watch, and believe me those boys were natural actors. The fight looked and sounded real. I ran to the kitchen window and loaded up an armload of burritos like you would carry an armload of wood, got back on the train and counted them, thirty-two for about six or seven of us.

For those of you who do not know any Spanish, I will explain. These things are made by putting a narrow ridge of beans, chopped goat meat, and chopped hot chili peppers across one side of a thin tough pancake like deal, then they

23

roll it into a round roll and pinch the ends together and bake it. They are wonderful eating, especially if you are a hungry hobo that has just crossed one of the meanest stretches of desert in the United States.

The train hadn't much more than gotten started before those cooks discovered what had happened, and you never heard so many "Ah hequella chingows, gringo cabrones, and chingow ti madres" in your life. You would have thought we were the worst people on earth.

The moral side is, I would not have done that if that little amigo would have given me one or two of those burritos and, moreover, it just goes to show that it doesn't pay to be stingy. There have been hoboes from every race, creed, and color in the world that have ridden the railroads and walked the highways of the United States, Canada, and Mexico, ever since the beginning of hoboism. I think if the hoboes have a Lord's chosen people it would be the Irish.

When I first started on the road in 1929, the majority of old-time genuine hoboes were Irish. Maybe that is the reason I adapted so easily to hobo life, for when you get right down to it, I am partly Irish, on both sides of the family or on both sides of the house, as the saying goes.

The old-time Irish hoboes rode trains when it was a rough and dangerous way to live, for in the early days and even down to my time it was necessary to ride the rods, brake rods underneath the cars, to keep from getting caught and thrown off the train, put in jail, or in many cases beaten up by some sadistic brakeman with a club.

All brakemen carry a hardwood club which they use in various ways in their job to help pull coupling pens, turn difficult brake wheels on top of the ends of cars, and to sprague the wheels of cars to slow them down, stop them, or keep a car or cut of cars from rolling.

This brakeman's club is quite similar to a baseball bat, except that they are flat on two sides, as opposed to being perfectly round like a ball bat.

A lot of professional hoboes carried a one-by-twelve-inch

board about six feet long to lie on when they were riding the rods. But let me tell you something, this was a rough way to travel. You laid on your belly on the board on top of the brake rods, which were only about a foot off the ground, and when the train was going fifty or sixty miles an hour it threw up a stream of cinders, sand, and small rocks, so if you rode a couple hundred miles you were almost beaten to death by the time you got off. My conscience is pretty clear on this score, as I only rode the rods twice and I'm sorry I punished myself even that much, in spite of the fact that in one instance I was definitely dodging a kill crazy railroad dick at Moberly, Missouri, on the Wabash main line between Kansas City and St. Louis. My other rod experience was on the Peavine, the Terre Haute to Peoria division of the old Pennsylvania Railroad.

Speaking of that rod board makes me think of a funny story. A bunch of us were sitting around the C.&E.I. jungle at Vincennes, Indiana, back during the Prohibition era and a few of the guys were drinking Jamaica Ginger, Bay Rum, Canned Heat, and anything else that had any alcohol in it, so they were pretty high and doing a lot of nutty talking. All of a sudden old Mungo Penman from Freedonia, Kansas, picked up an old paper sack off the ground, dug around in his pockets, and found a stub pencil and started writing, using his knee for a desk. "Farmer Jim" Bailey asked what he was writing. Mungo said, "Farmer, I'm making out my will, and you are my sole beneficiary."

Farmer asked, "What in the world have you got that anyone would want?"

Mungo said, "I'll tell you what I've got, I've got the only upholstered rod board in the United States. It is completely covered with burlap sacks, so that it is reversible and you can use either side. When I pass on it is all yours."

Farmer asked, "Where is that upholstered board?"

Mungo said, "I've got it hid behind that tile plant up there at Brazil."

Farmer asked, "How will I find it? That's a big tile plant."

25

Mungo told him, "When I die, look in my left sock and you'll find a map."

Then Farmer said, "Hey Mung, include that can of heat you've got in your coat pocket, just in case you pass on quicker than we expect."

Many of those guys were World War One veterans, and about 98 percent of these hobo veterans were "boosters," or, in conventional terms, hopeless drunks. They are all dead now and most of them died easy. They just lie down someplace and go to sleep and don't wake up, and you can't beat that.

MUNGO SHAVING THE TRAMP

Mungo was a barber when he was in the army, and a good one, even when he was drunk. Mung and I got off a C.&E.I. freight train down in Sullivan, Indiana, one time and went down to the jungle to check on the accommodations and facilities and arrived just in time to see a guy trying to shave with a piece of broken catsup bottle.

Mungo carried a straight razor suspended on a whang leather shoestring around his neck and the razor reposing on his chest under his shirt. He took a look at the guy and said, "Hell, buddy, I'll shave you. You could cut your head off with that broken bottle." Then he took his razor out and started stropping it on the palm of his hand. He told the guy to soap his face up good, then he stepped over and placed his left hand on the top of the man's head and started the razor at the bottom of the sideburn and swish, he dropped it off the point of the man's chin with one clean sweep, the man's knees banged together a couple times and he said, "Aw hell, man, you're going to cut my head off."

Mungo said, "Sit still, boy, I ain't gonna hurt you." He still had hold of the guy's head so he laid the razor against the other sideburn and swish, down the jaw and off the chin, then he slowed down a little and finished shaving the man, who by this time was scared stiff. He was using the bottom of a new tin can for a mirror so he looked at himself and run his hand over his face.

Mungo asked, "How does that shave suit you?"

The man said, "That's a good shave, but it's the last damned time any drunk ever shaves me in a hobo jungle or anywhere else."

BACON BUTTS

Another incident that happened in southern Indiana years ago that I shall never forget was when Pat Kincaid was hit by a Standard Oil truck.

A couple of buddies of mine, Elmer Stone and Pat Kincaid and I got off a train at Princeton, Indiana, one morning and decided to try to round up some groceries and jungle up for two or three days. At that time Princeton had a good-sized hobo jungle at the south edge of town, along the west side of the C.&E.I. railroad right of way.

We planned our strategy and headed for the uptown business district to work the stem, as they say in the lingo of the road. Pat was to get some bacon for seasoning, and Stony was to get some "punk" and toppings (bread and pastry), and I was to get the fruit, vegetables, and condiments.

Within an hour Pat had all his pockets full of little packages of bacon scraps, butts, and bacon skins, so he headed for the jungle. As he was crossing a street a Standard Oil truck hit him and knocked him about fifteen feet, end over end. The little packs of bacon flew all over the street. Pat was about five feet ten inches and weighed 250 pounds and this hog muscle is probably what saved his life. He was skinned and bruised but otherwise unhurt. They took him to a hospital and doctored him up and let him go.

The day after Pat got run over the paper headlines read: "Standard Oil Truck Hits Pork Trust." Stony and I gave him the permanent name of Bacon Butts, and in due time he was known far and wide by that name, and few if any ever called him Pat.

These men have long since gone to that Big Jungle in the sky, and I hope the Lord is as fond of them as I was, for they were a couple of fine human beings.

THE FIRST OGDEN FIASCO

I had a hair-raising experience in Ogden, Utah, one evening. I was downtown trying to promote a nice "set down" in some friendly restaurant when up came a squad car and some unfriendly cop asked, "What are you doing, panhandling?"

I said, "Well, sir, I think some people do call it that, but in reality I am trying to find someone who will trade me some food for a little work."

He said, "Get in here, wise guy, and I'll give you a choice. Either get out of Ogden or go to jail." I got into the squad car and they took me out to the U.P. yards and told me, "Catch the first thing that goes out of here and scram, for if I see you around here anymore I'll put you in the clink."

When we got to the yards there was a redball fruit express icing up. They always have to ice up the refrigerator cars' iceboxes after they cross that desert. This train was heading east and since these people were so unfriendly I had a feeling that I should head for Chicago, where the public servants weren't so damned nosy.

I walked down the track a couple of hundred feet ahead of the lead engine and decided to wait there and catch the train about fifteen cars back of the engine and get out of the diesel fumes, as I would have to ride the top of that redball. If you get too far forward or too far back those fumes are murder.

I was standing there waiting to hear that high ball when up came a big railroad dick and asked, "Are you figuring on catching that train?"

I said, "Yes."

He said, "No, you're not, I'll see that you don't ride that one."

I asked, "Why can't I ride that train?"

He said, "I'll tell you why, first of all it's a redball, solid

29

fruit express, and secondly it's a hundred and five miles from here to Evanston, Wyoming and there's twenty-nine tunnels between here and Evanston, and one of them is two and a half miles long."

I asked, "Which is the long tunnel?"

He said, "It's the seventh tunnel from here."

I said, "Thank you, sir."

Then he said, "Come on, let's walk down the track aways and I'm sure you won't get it when it comes by."

In those high mountains they use Malley diesels (mountain engines), and they use two engines to each freight train and I have even seen them use a lead engine and a kicker on passenger trains in some extremely high, steep mountain grades. It doesn't take those mountain Malleys long to get a train moving, and that's what this dick was counting on.

When the lead engine went by us I listened to the exhaust, and it was beginning to come pretty short and keen, so I knew that if I was ever going to get that train I had to get it now. I asked, "Mr. Dick, if I can get it, do I have your permission?"

He said, "Yes, but you ain't going to get it now, it is running forty-five or fifty miles an hour."

I took off as fast as I could run and those cars were passing me like bullets and just for a moment even I thought to myself, I can't do it, then I reached for a grab iron and my hand closed around it and I hung on. The momentum of the train jerked me off my feet and threw my feet up in the air and they hit the top of the car, but I hung on to that grab iron. My feet and body came down and my feet landed squarely in the stirrup and skinned my shins from my ankles to my knees.

The instant I realized that I had made it, I turned and waved good-bye to old Dick. He just stood there and shook his head in disbelief. But that really wasn't anything when you consider that the great athlete, Indian Jim Thorpe, could get on and off trains that were running sixty or sixty-five miles per hour.

As we climbed higher and higher into the Rockies I counted

the tunnels as we made them, and when we were approaching number seven I lay down on the catwalk and unbuckled my belt and rebuckled it around one of those one-by-three boards so that I couldn't fall off, even if the fumes knocked me out when we were going through that long tunnel.

That dick had told me that two guys had gotten asphyxiated on that same train the night before and had fallen off the top and been ground up like hamburger in that long tunnel. I didn't plan to join them nor duplicate their ignorance and inexperience.

As we went into the tunnel I inhaled as deeply as I could and held my breath as long as I could and hoped we were more than halfway through the tunnel, then I exhaled and held my breath again and before long we came out the other end of the tunnel and I really grabbed some lungs full of that fresh mountain air, and thought to myself, "Well, that was rough, but it was worth it to get out of Ogden."

FROM ST. LOUIS TO MONET

I have ridden nearly every railroad in the United States and Canada and three or four different ones in Mexico, and I have ridden narrow gauge railroads with wood-burning engines and I saw one or two narrow gauge lines with gear driven engines, but the most unusual line I ever rode was the old Iron Mountain Railroad that ran from St. Louis in a southwesterly direction to Little Rock, Arkansas, and I don't know where it went from there.

One of my old road buddies Jack Ross and I caught a rattler out of St. Louis on the Iron Mountain and rode all day and finally made it to Monet, Missouri, about 7:30 that evening. We had left St. Louis (Saint Louie, as a lot of those old boys called it) about 8:00 A.M. so we were eleven hours, making about 150 or 175 miles.

Old Jack was killed at St. Lo, France, in 1944, but if he was here he would verify this story. This train was made up of ore cars going to the lead minefield around Monet. This train stopped at every town between St. Louis and Monet. The crew would get off and stand there and talk to various people for fifteen or twenty minutes, then climb back on the train, blow a high ball, and go another four or five or six or eight miles and stop for some reason. Twice they stopped and carried water from a creek in buckets and put it in the water tank and went on down the line.

They stopped at a creek at noon, took their lunch buckets, and went down on the creek bank under some shade trees and ate and talked for nearly an hour. Jack and I went down to see what was so interesting in that creek, for they just kept pointing and talking about something. They were talking about coming down there fishing and frog hunting sometime. Believe me, that creek was literally full of nice fish and the biggest bullfrogs I ever saw.

It was a long tiresome ride, for any type of a gondola car is hard riding, but truthfully we enjoyed it, for in reality it was an eleven-hour scenic tour through the good old state of Missouri. There is one place in the United States that is undoubtedly the most primitive place on this continent, and that is the swamp country of south Arkansas.

I came out of Memphis, Tennessee, one time, crossed the Mississippi River on the road to Little Rock. I was riding along taking in all the scenery when all of a sudden we came into the most prehistoric mile after mile of swamps, filled with a multitude of birds of all sizes and colors, snakes large enough to swallow a full-grown chicken, and flathead catfish that were unbelievable.

The railroad was on a manmade roadbed about ten to twelve feet high, commonly known as a grade. I could sit there in that boxcar door and look right down into that shallow water and see all those marine monsters leisurely swimming around next to the base of the grade.

Before long we came to a cypress swamp about twenty-five or thirty miles long. What a sight, millions of cypress knees as far as the eye could see in any direction, except right down the center of that railroad. These knees looked like countless big ice cream cones turned upside down in the water. Over the years I went back and forth through this swamp country and I never ceased to marvel at it.

CLIMBING SHERMAN HILL

I hear an echo from the past
Though the night is very still,
A compound Malley on a manifest
Pulling up Sherman Hill.

This hill is the trademark of old Cheyenne
As every bo doth know,
A beautiful sight at sunrise
In the morning's golden glow.

In the distance I see a little fire
Along the U.P. main,
Some hobo's camp by the water tower
Where he'll catch a westbound train.

Then I hear that lonesome whistle
As that Malley tops the hill
And heads on west to the sawtooth's
In the early morning chill.

COTTON PICKER HUNTER

I came into east Little Rock one evening and when the train slowed down as it entered the yards I got off and headed for a nearby street. I was thinking about where I would go and where I would spend the night. A big railroad dick stepped out from behind a telephone box and quickly solved these problems. He put his hand on that big .38 Colt and said, "Hold it boy! Don't you know it is against the law to ride those trains?"

I said, "No, I didn't."

He said, "Well, that eleven months and twenty-nine days on Tucker Farm pulling a cotton sack will teach you a few things."

I had heard about Tucker Farm a hundred times and it had the worst reputation of any penal institution in the United States. This was revealed to the general public a few years ago when they started that big investigation that disclosed all those dead bodies of men that had been murdered by the guards and other officials at Tucker Farm over a period of many years and buried in unmarked graves here and there over this disgraceful farm.

On that trip down to the famous Pulaski County jail I must have felt like people do when they are heading for the gallows or electric chair. My heart just seemed to die within my chest. I asked the detective to shoot me and get it over with quick. He just laughed and said, "No, boy, I don't aim to do anything to make it easy on you."

It is hard, cruel, and unjust to be treated like a criminal when you haven't done anything to deserve it. He took me down to the jail and booked me, and they threw me in the drunk tank with two or three other hoboes and four or five town drunks.

The next morning they took all of us "criminals" over to

35

the city court and the judge began immediately to hand out sentences, which ranged from five days in the county jail to eleven to twenty-nine at Tucker Farm.

My heart was beating like a trip-hammer and there was a cold sweat over my entire body. The judge called my name and I walked up and stood before him. He said, "You are charged with hoboing, riding trains without permission, and trespassing on private property [the railroad]. How do you plead, guilty or not guilty?"

I said, "Judge, I am not really a hobo, I was born and raised on a small farm in central Indiana. My father died when I was fourteen years old and I had to step in and do my best to take his place, which naturally I could not do. Now my mother is sick and in constant pain with a tumor of some kind and needs surgery, but we didn't have the money. I heard that you could get a job just about anyplace in Little Rock, Arkansas, so I got on a train and came down here to try to help my mother. That is how it is, Your Honor, and I most surely didn't intend to break any laws, so I would appreciate it very much if you would give me a break."

He studied this over for a few moments, then he asked, "Can you prove what you are telling me?"

I said, "Yes, sir, and I'll be glad to give you these phone numbers so you can check on me and my story."

He looked intently into my face for what seemed like five minutes, then he said, "Young man, I seldom let anyone off scot-free, but I think you are telling the truth. I will have the police take you out to the east city limit of Little Rock and put you on the highway and you had better be out of Arkansas by four o'clock this evening. Moreover, if I ever see you in my courtroom again I'll give you the same eleven to twenty-nine that I should give you now."

I thanked him and said, "Judge, I won't let you down, in any respect, for I hope to be out of Arkansas by 3:00 P.M. at the very latest, and I am not coming back."

Those cops were just plain nasty all the way out to the city limit, so I kept my mouth shut, for I knew what they were angling for.

I was well aware of the fact that they always needed help down on Tucker Farm, and they were miffed because that judge gave me a break.

I started walking east as soon as I got out of the car, for I wanted to get as far away from that corporation boundary as I could. I had only walked about two city blocks when a drummer (traveling salesman) came along and picked me up.

I told him my story and he said, "To hell with them, we will eat supper in St. Louis if nothing happens." So it was that we were sitting in a restaurant in Kirkwood, Missouri, at 5:45 P.M. eating. What a relief, now I knew what it felt like to go through hell backwards, as the saying goes. Let me assure you that it was several years before I went back to Arkansas and then only when I had a car to drive and money in my pocket.

THE THREE-INCH DROP

Once when I was out in Nebraska a brakeman, or brakey, put me off a train when we stopped on a siding to let a passenger train go by. This siding was miles from any town so I prepared for a long walk alone and at night. Such is the life of a hobo.

The train pulled out and Mr. Brakey stood right there with me until the caboose, or crummy, came by and he grabbed it and climbed aboard, and I was alone.

I started walking and before long it started drizzling rain and began to get dark early. I went on and when darkness came it was as black as the bottom of a skillet.

I stayed in the middle of the track and tried to step from tie to tie, by guess. I couldn't find anyplace to get into for the night so I just kept walking. I probably crossed half a dozen little bridges and cement culverts without knowing it and maybe even passed an old deserted house or two.

Later on I came to a long iron bridge that I knew must cross a pretty good-sized stream. I could just barely make out the huge iron frame above me, so I started to cross that bridge and hoping there were no ties missing, making a hole that I might fall through and be killed.

When I was perhaps midway off the bridge I saw the headlight of an approaching train. I tried to hurry and get off the bridge before the train got there, but not being able to see I couldn't make much headway. Before long I realized that I was going to have to get down over the side of the bridge or be killed. I sat down on the end of the cross ties and felt around with my foot until I found a tie-rod, then I eased myself down onto it while holding onto the ball of the rail. As the train drew nearer I could see that in order to balance myself on that tie-rod I would have to hold to the end of the ties and this would put my head almost under the side of the train, and that was too dangerous.

I held onto a tie and squatted down and grasped the tie-rod with my left hand and steadied myself as best I could and brought my right hand down and clamped it onto the tie-rod. I couldn't balance myself there so I swung my body down over the rod and hung there by my hands. I intended to pull myself back up on the rod and climb back up on the bridge when the train got by. As luck would have it, that freight train must have been a mile long and by the time it got by my arms were too tired to pull me back up on the tie-rod. There was nothing I could do but hang on as long as I could and postpone the inevitable.

I tried several times to throw my legs up around the tie-rod, but each try just made my hands and arms that much more exhausted and helpless. I knew before long I would have to let go and drop, how far and into what? Was the water deep and free of rocks and pilings and other objects that would mean almost sure death? Was the water so shallow that I would break both legs when I landed, and perhaps drown in eighteen inches or two feet of water? All of these things passed through my mind as I hung there and I put in a thousand years of mental anguish in perhaps twenty-five minutes.

Finally I had to let go, and it was then that I experienced the greatest shock of my entire life. In my dash to beat that train to the end of the bridge I had gotten much farther along than I thought, so when I dropped I only fell about two or three inches and landed firmly on a nice firm riverbank about twenty feet back from the edge of the water.

The sudden switch from an expected death or severe injury to total safety was almost too much for my heart. I could hardly breathe for two or three minutes and I became so weak that I had to sit down and remain quiet for perhaps an hour or more.

GHOST TOWN KILLER

During my years on the road I narrowly escaped death on a number of occasions but only once did I stick my neck out and invite disaster. The following story is it.

I and a buddy of mine, Alex Kachinske of Escanaba, Michigan, caught a train out of Lincoln, Nebraska, one time and we were worse than a couple of rank amateurs. We were a disgrace to the hobo philosophy. On the spur of the moment we grabbed a train that was made up of nothing but sand cars, and we should have known that they were not going any farther than some big sand pit. I never heard of Sandoval, Nebraska until that day, but that is where the sand pit was, and that is where they set off all of those sand cars, hooked onto the caboose, and headed back for Lincoln.

I asked the brakeman how far it was to the next town? He said, "That is Plattsmouth and it is twenty-six miles east of here."

The Polski and I walked every step of that twenty-six miles, rough miles. That Alex was one of the best buddies a man ever had. About halfway to Plattsmouth we came to a ghost town, it was pitch dark and there was a storm coming up. There were several cattle cars on the siding at this ghost town, and as we walked along beside the cattle cars we heard a human voice asking, "Hey! Have you got a cigarette on you?" We stopped and I said, "Yes, I have a cigarette, but where are you?"

"Up here in this car," he said. Then he jumped down on the ground and I handed him a bag of Dukes Mixture and struck matches and held a light while he rolled a cigarette. I saw a man with the meanest face I had ever seen in my life.

I lit the cigarette for him and he took a drag or two, then he asked, "Where did you guys come from?"

"We came from Lincoln," we said.

Then he asked, "Did there seem to be much money around there?"

I said, "Hell, man, we are hoboes, how would we know who had money and who didn't?"

He said, "Let's all go back there and I'll find out where the money is, and if they don't give it to me I will kill them."

We told him "No, we aren't interested in anything like that."

Then he asked, "Where are you going now?"

We told him to Plattsmouth.

He said, "OK, I'm going with you." I told him that he had better stay where he was and keep out of trouble. He really unloaded then, He said, "I escaped from Kansas state prison two weeks ago, after serving fourteen years in that damned hole for murder. I was doing a double life sentence and no one is ever going to take me back and I don't intend to be broke and hungry, even if I have to kill all the people I meet."

I realized that Alex and I might be in for some trouble, but I didn't really know what to do.

I said again, "Buddy, you had better stay here, where you are pretty safe."

He said, "No, I'm going with you guys!"

We started walking east and sure enough he came along. Alex was walking next to me and I got an idea. I said, "Alex, why don't you walk on the other side of old buddy Kansas?"

He said OK and moved over. It was dark so I took my pocketknife out and opened the little blade. Our buddy Kansas was the only thing I could see, for his white shirt was visible even in the dark.

I finally got up the nerve to make my move. I pressed the point of that little blade against his ribs and said, "Well, Mr. Kansas, you either turn back now to your cattle cars or I am going to kill you." He was noticeably shocked at the sudden turn of events for he said, "Be careful there, you are going to cut me! I was just trying to help you guys."

I said, "You heard me, scram. We don't want none of your goddamned help and if you don't go now I will leave you lying here in two pieces."

41

And I meant it, for my nature is such that I can only get so scared, then I get a little dangerous.

Alex and I had walked perhaps half a mile when all of a sudden I got so scared I could hardly walk. I mentioned it to him and he said, "So am I."

The storm was getting closer and the lightning flashes were getting closer together so I told Alex, "Watch behind us when that lightning flashes and if we see that white shirt coming, we will head for the woods and hide."

Thank the Lord, we never saw the white shirt man again. We walked on toward Plattsmouth and the storm broke in all its fury and we were soaking wet before we hardly had time to move. Alex asked, "What will we do now?"

I said, "There isn't much we can do, only keep on walking and hope we don't get hit by lightning or drowned before we get to Plattsmouth."

We reached Plattsmouth about midnight, soaking wet, dog tired, hungry, and discouraged. The lightning showed us two boxcars sitting on a hill by the local grain elevator, and they were both empty and had the doors partly open.

How lucky we were to find these cars on that hill! There were three or four guys in the car we climbed into and one of them had some dry tobacco and matches. We mooched him out of a couple cigarettes and after we smoked we lay down and slept the sleep of the just or of the tired.

We awoke around eight or nine o'clock and got out of the car and looked around. You couldn't believe it, this town was on the Missouri River and that storm had been a cloudburst so the town was inundated.

The river was so high the water was up to the eaves of the houses, with women letting babies nurse, and there were goats, chickens, dogs, cats, and people on every roof.

I noticed all you could see of the railroad trestle were the tops, or balls, of the rails. The hills across the river in Iowa looked good, so I began toying with the idea of crossing that flooded river some way. I knew if Alex and I crouched down and held onto the balls of those rails we could make it across, unless the bridge suddenly collapsed and washed out, as they sometimes do.

I told him what I was thinking, and he asked, "Do you think we can make it?"

I said, "Yes, at least it is worth a try, as I'm getting pretty hungry."

He said, "OK, I'm ready when you are."

I cautioned him to hang on tightly to the rails if we came to a place where a tie or two were missing, and I told him that I would take the lead, all he had to do was follow me, but if I go down and disappear you go back to that hill and wait for the flood to go down.

We made it across and not without a lot of risk and some difficulty.

We put our shoes and socks on and rolled our pant legs down and started walking up a little gravel road. A couple of miles from the river we came to the town of Pacific Junction, Iowa, and as we were walking down the main drag we met the marshal. He was a little man about 5 feet 4 inches and weighed perhaps 120 pounds. He had a walrus mustache and was carrying a .45 six-shooter that looked nearly as big as he was. But he turned out to be a real nice guy. He said, "Hi, boys, where did you come from?" We told him Plattsmouth, Nebraska, and he said, "You are joking, how could you get across that river?"

We told him and he said, "That takes more nerve than I've got." Then he said, "I don't allow any panhandling in this town, but if you're hungry I will take you down to the restaurant and buy you a meal."

We accepted his offer with pleasure and followed him down to the restaurant. He said, "Order whatever you want, boys."

We did, and would you believe we were heroes before the man could get our food out there. That's right, the old marshal announced to everyone in there, "Here are two of the bravest men you ever met." Then he started telling them about how we had crossed the Missouri River in the worst flood that he had ever seen.

After we had eaten and were thanking the marshal for his kindness and preparing to leave, the man that ran the restaurant said, "I think we should take up a collection and give it to these boys, for they have showed this town what real courage is."

We got about five dollars from the collection and thanked everyone, and the marshal and us walked outside. He said, "Anytime you boys hit town, hunt me up and I'll see that you get all you can eat and some cigarettes." Then he said, "By the way, I forgot to ask you about cigarettes while we were in there, what kind do you smoke?" We told him and a couple of minutes later he was back with four packs of cigarettes and two boxes of safety matches for us. We thanked him again and left.

About a year later I went through there again and inquired about the marshal and was told that he had died about six months before. I am convinced that people like that will get a reward in heaven, for I think the Lord will give special consideration to folks like that little old marshal. He was straight out hard and tough, but he was fair and honest.

HAIR TONIC

I have done several mysterious things in my life that lead me to believe that I just might be the original invisible man.

One chilly October night I was sleeping in a boxcar with five or six other men at Terre Haute, Indiana. The car was sitting on a switch track at the Continental Can Company on the banks of the Wabash. There was about ten or twelve inches of straw all over the floor of the car, so we were bedded down as snug as a bug in a rug. A straw hobo bed is simple but very comfortable even in relatively cold weather. All you have to do is lie down and rake some straw over you from each side.

On this particular night we were all strawed over and sound asleep when all of a sudden someone started yelling and cursing and when we all sat up we were looking at two glaring flashlights and down the barrels of two .38s with two apparently angry or mad men behind them. I have often wondered if some of these characters were not mad at the world when they were born.

These men started shouting questions at the hoboes nearest to them. The first man said he was from New York and sold hair tonic for a living. Then they asked another man his name and where he was from. He was either drunk or so stupid he couldn't even answer a simple question, so they went back to the first man and I heard one of them yell, "Hey, hair tonic, bla, bla, bla." At this moment something seemed to tell me to get up and slip along the opposite wall and go through the open door, drop to the ground, and leave. And like an invisible robot I did just that. I went right in front of those men and they didn't see me. I went down on the riverbank and hid behind a rock wall where I wouldn't or shouldn't be annoyed by any more wild men that night. The bad part was I had been obliged to trade a good warm bed for a cold sandy riverbank, but such is life.

WILD WHEAT

One time Jack Ross and I took a job working in the wheat harvest. This old farmer said he would give us fifty cents a day and our board and room, which was about normal wages for the times. We went to bed about 9:00 P.M. in an upstairs room that had been assigned to us. It wasn't too long before the old man was up there shaking us and saying, "Come on, boys, it is time to get up, we want to get an early start on cutting that wheat."

We sat up in bed and Jack asked, "What time is it?" The farmer said, "It is two o'clock, be three before we can get our breakfast and get to the field."

Jack always had an answer, so he said, "Hell, man, if that wheat is so wild that we've got to slip up on it in the dark, I don't want any part of it. Me and the chief will get up about six o'clock and get a bite of breakfast and head on down the road, for we can't work for anyone that has to get up at two A.M. to make a living."

Boy! was that old man mad. He said, "OK, you ain't no damned good anyway, I'll give you a night's lodging and a free supper and breakfast just to get rid of you."

Jack always called me Chief because of my Indian ancestry and that old man said, "If I had known that your buddy was an Indian I wouldn't have hired him in the first place." Then he went stomping and cursing down the stairs and we went back to sleep. We invited the old man to eat breakfast with us and it offended him.

He said, "It will be a cold day in July before I ever eat with the likes of you guys."

This Jack Ross was something else, it is men like him that make history.

CHICKEN DUMPLINGS

One time Jack and I were in Sikeston, Missouri, and he met a first cousin of his from Harrison, Arkansas. We visited awhile and decided to go home with him for a few days and visit the kinfolks. This man's mother was a sister to Jack's mother. These folks lived on a little farm outside of Harrison and when we got there we all had one big gab fest after I had been introduced to everyone.

Finally, Jack's cousin said, "I'd love to have a big pot of chicken and dumplings."

His dad said, "So would I. Why don't you boys slip up to Tom Brown's house tonight and swipe a couple of his big old fat hens and tomorrow Mom can fix them with dumplings and we'll have them for dinner."

He hated Tom Brown and jumped at the chance to do him some dirt, as they say down there. When night came, Jack and his cousin went to get the chickens and when they got outside the house his cousin said, "The old man has five or six hundred chickens so we will just circle around and come up behind his hen house and get a couple hens and he won't know the difference."

The next day we had a big pot of chicken and dumplings and the old man had a perpetual grin on his face all the time he was eating.

When we had finished eating he said, "I didn't know old Tom Brown raised such good chickens! I'll bet he would raise hell if he knew that we had eaten a couple of his nicest hens. Haw, Haw!" The old man lived out his life believing that he had, at least in part, gotten even with old Tom Brown.

I can truthfully say that the only thing I have ever stolen was something to eat and fuel to keep warm, and I don't regret that. Under the same circumstances I would do it again, for I think anyone would have to be mentally unbalanced if they went hungry or starved in a world that is so full of food.

I can also say that I have never hurt anyone who didn't try to hurt me first. And I don't regret anything that I have ever done to defend myself or a relative or friend that was being threatened, for self-preservation is the first law of nature.

THE MINNESOTA KILLER

I had a rather hectic experience up in northern Utah one time. I was riding on top of a loaded boxcar and got sleepy, so I laid down and buckled my belt around one of the one-by-three boards on the runway so I wouldn't fall off the train while I was sleeping. I was awakened by someone trying to unbuckle my belt, and though I was lying on my side and still fastened to the board, I did manage to punch him a couple of times. Then he jumped on top of me and tried to choke me.

A big young man from the East who was also on the car with us dashed over and said, "I'll take care of him, buddy."

He grabbed this guy by the shirt collar and held him so he wouldn't fall off the train and beat him into a pulp with that other hand.

I finally begged him to quit before he killed the man, and he asked, "What the hell do you think he was trying to do to you?" He slammed the guy down on the catwalk and gave him orders to sit there and leave people alone or I'll kill you the next time."

Some time later we came to a small town and the train stopped to set out, or pick up some cars, so we saw a fountain by the side of the street that ran parallel to the railroad and decided to get a drink while we had the chance.

We all climbed down and headed for the fountain. Someone said, "To keep everyone honest let's just line up and take our turn at the fountain."

We lined up and when I got to the fountain I bent over to get a drink and, BANG! Someone hit me on the back of the head and knocked my mouth against the centerpiece in that fountain and split my lips and the blood flew.

I beat this mean character all over that street and back and just kept hammering him until the train was getting ready to leave, then I grabbed a quick drink, blood and all, and caught the train and left old meany lying there on the ground. I thought that would be the last time any of us would ever see him. But, lo and behold, a few miles out of town he came walking on the top of the train and sat down by us. By this time I was beginning to wonder what kind of a man this was that you couldn't hurt or scare.

Before long we stopped in another town and were met by two railroad detectives and a U.S. marshal who made us all get down on the ground and line up. The lawmen walked down the line and looked closely at each man, then said, "OK, go."

Finally they came to old meany and I heard one of them say, "That's him, put your hands up high!" They searched him, then put handcuffs on him and took him away.

I finally got a chance to talk to one of those railroad dicks, so I asked him what the man had done.

He said, "He is an escaped mental patient from Minnesota. He was serving time for killing three or four people with a corn knife. Every law man in the West has been hunting him for almost a year. It is a miracle that he didn't kill one of you guys, he is a bad one. We got a tip that he was on that train, and this tip wasn't a crackpot joke."

I never saw the Minnesota psycho again and all I can say is, thank God.

BEEG SNEEK PEEK LIL BOY

I took a job on the Texas Pacific Railroad working on a track gang west of El Paso, Texas, swinging a spike mall with a Mexican wetback from Monterrey, Mexico. The gang was made up of nineteen or twenty Mexicans, an Italian boss, and I.

The boss spoke very bad English and only two of the Mexicans could speak any English and that was very limited and very poor. I had a time trying to communicate with them so I was happy when I got laid off at the end of two weeks.

There were some camp cars parked about a quarter of a mile west of where I stayed, and those cars were for married people, some of whom had two or three children. The cars on the east end was for single men and housed the kitchen and dining room.

One evening, about a week after I started to work there, a Mexican from the family cars by the name of Roberto Hernandes came running with a little boy and told me, "Beeg sneek peek lil boy." I said, "You mean a big snake bit the little boy." He said, "Si."

I told him to see the honcho and take the boy to town to a doctor. I tried to tell him in Spanish. "Vamose to el ciudad, meda el doc-tore."

He got my meaning and said, "Gracias, amigo."

He laid the boy on the porch when I showed him in sign language, and while he went to get the boss I put a rag tourniquet on the boy's leg just below the knee, for the snake bite was an inch or two above his ankle.

When Roberto and the boss came back I showed them how to work the tourniquet and they jumped into the boss's old 1924 Dodge touring car and headed for town.

The boy was in bed for two or three days and came out of his ordeal OK.

None of us actually saw the snake, but I imagine it was either a diamondback or a sidewinder "horned" rattlesnake, for those dudes were pretty numerous in spots here and there in that country.

PRICKLY PEARS
AND BARREL CACTUS

I was hitchhiking west through Arizona on Route 80 on my way to the coast when I spotted a big patch of ripe prickly pears, or cactus apples, as they are called in some areas. I showed them to the folks I was riding with and the man stopped the car and we all got out and headed for the cactus patch.

These folks said they had never eaten any prickly pears but were eager to try them. Each of us ate five or six of the reddish purple fruits apiece, got back in the car, and went on. We camped that night at the butt of a butte along the south side of the road. We all rolled up in blankets on the sand and went to sleep. I awoke about midnight and I had troubles, for I was so sick that I thought I was going to die. Within two minutes I had to vomit and go to the toilet at the same time. I jumped up and ran about a hundred feet from camp and let go at both ends at the same time and repeated this every five minutes for two hours until I was so weak I could hardly walk.

When the crisis had passed I rolled up in the blanket again and went back to sleep. I had only slept a few minutes when something hit me and I thought a mountain lion had attacked me, as I was hurting all over. When I got up and looked I saw a large barrel cactus lying there. Thank the Lord, there was a half-moon shining and it was nearly as light as day.

My yelling and moaning awakened my companions and they came to my rescue. The man discovered my back and buttocks were full of cactus spines about an inch and a half long. He tried to pull one out with his fingers but it wouldn't budge, then he got a pair of pliers and started in, and each time he pulled one I yelled so loud you could have heard me for five miles. Those spines have a hook on the side, right above the point and those hooks are what hurt so bad.

That was some night. The prickly pears had poisoned me and the barrel cactus had broken loose from the side of that butte and rolled down and nearly killed me. That just wasn't my day. Needless to say I was pretty puny for two or three weeks.

THE GYP WATER

On another occasion these same people and I pulled into Hassayampa, Arizona, thirsty and tired and the canteens nearly empty.

I spotted a fountain in front of a big garage in the uptown area of the town, so I jumped out of the car and asked the proprietor if we could have some water.

He said, "Yes, sir, help yourself. Take all you want."

I should have suspected something, but I didn't. I do know that no one in the Arizona desert gives drinking water away for free. I have paid ten cents a glass for water in restaurants many times and twenty-five cents for a canteen of drinking water right at the well.

I told these folks to come on and get all the water they wanted. While they were getting out of the car I grabbed a quick drink and it was cold and good. They all drank, then I took a second and bigger drink and shortly they all took a second drink. We filled the canteens and checked the radiator, got our gas tank filled, then took off again through the desert. We were happy and grateful for meeting such a generous man.

We had only gone about twenty-five or thirty miles when a pain hit me in the belly and I said, "Stop the car, quick!" I just had time to run behind the car and drop my pants. I got back into the car and before we could leave one of the others had to go behind the car, then another and another until all had been out behind the car. We drove five or six miles and repeated the procedure. In fact, we were normally modest, but before long modesty went out the window, for at various times two or three of us were out there at once unashamedly having a bowel movement.

In the next town we all visited the toilets at a filling station one right after another. I mentioned our problem to the operator and he asked, "Did you drink some water at a garage and filling station in Hassayampa?"

I said, "Yes, and we filled our canteens. Why?"

He laughed and said, "That sucker does that to every tourist that comes through there and asks for water, that is a big joke with him. That is gyp water, and it is worse than Epsom salts if you wasn't born and raised around there!"

He let us empty our canteens and refill them with regular water and only charged us fifty cents for the three canteens.

We had all recovered from our diarrhea by nightfall and went to sleep happy that it was over and much wiser for our experience. We would most surely be on the alert for gyp water from now on.

THE SIDEWINDER

On another occasion, I was crossing the same Arizona desert with an old tramp cowboy that I had got acquainted with back East.

We stopped in Globe, Arizona, and dinged some groceries, then we walked two or three miles west of town and finally found a suitable camping spot. We had mooched a gallon of water and had it in a one-gallon syrup bucket that we had found behind a restaurant and washed out for this purpose. We found a place where there was a lot of dead cactus to use for firewood and my cowboy buddy, Hyman, and I were both hungry so we set up housekeeping in a hurry. Hyman said, "If you will build a fire, I will cook supper." He had a small sheet iron skillet and a small coffee pot in his bedroll, so we could live like the folks uptown, as far as cooking was concerned. I had been told a hundred times to never pick up anything in the desert without kicking it over a foot or two to make sure there was nothing under it. Even Hyman had told me half a dozen times about the time he carelessly grabbed up an old newspaper and got stung on the hand by a scorpion. I was in a hurry to get a fire started so I grabbed a piece of cactus too quick.

I saw something move and I jerked my hand back as quick as I could, but he hit me a pretty good lick anyway. I looked down and there was a little sidewinder, a horned rattlesnake, about twelve or fourteen inches long. Since the largest sidewinder is not over eighteen inches long, this wasn't a baby. It was a full-grown snake. I looked at my hand and saw two places that were bleeding a little and starting to hurt. I cursed that snake and even talked about his mother. Then old Hyman came over there and said, "Let's see how bad he got you."

I wiped the blood off with my handkerchief and there

were two little bluish-looking holes in my right hand near the thumb.

Hyman chewed tobacco, so he took a big chew out of his mouth and put it on the snake bite, then tied my handkerchief around my hand to hold the tobacco in place.

He said, "Leave that on until morning and we'll look at it and see how it is coming along."

The next morning he took the handkerchief off and the tobacco was as green as grass. The snake bite left scars that I have to this day, but it didn't even get sore, thanks to old Hyman's tobacco.

THE BROWNSVILLE BULL

I came into Brownsville, Texas, one time and found some kind of a fair or big celebration going on and I knew my chances of eating were pretty good. I was walking down the main drag and came upon a regulation prize ring and a man was announcing that he would give anyone two dollars that would stay with Poncho for three rounds. I looked Poncho over and decided that I would try to collect that two bucks.

No one had any extra ring shoes or trunks or anything else, so I had to box old Poncho in my bare feet, street pants, with no wrappings for my hands, and we were using eight-ounce gloves.

Poncho was a bull, so for two rounds I made him miss, tied him up, and managed to stay in there. The third round I decided to mix it up and see if he really could fight. Don't ever sell a Mexican short. They are tough and game. I was glad when that was over and I'm even more glad that I didn't try to stand toe to toe and fight him those first two rounds, for I needed that two dollars.

After the fight was over I collected my two dollars and was putting my shoes on when some man and his wife came up to me and asked me if I would like to go to a nice restaurant and get a big steak dinner with all the trimmings?

I thanked them and explained that I wasn't dressed to go to a very nice restaurant and moreover I had some money of my own to eat on now.

The man said, "We enjoyed that fight and just want to do something nice for you, and you can keep your two dollars for later."

I said, "OK, but I hope I don't embarrass you."

We got in their car and went out on the highway that led to El Paso. A mile or so west of town there was a big restaurant, a casino that had anything you wanted if you had the money to buy it.

We dined in style and I found these folks to be real nice people. I wasn't used to that kind of chow, but I somehow managed to survive this pleasant experience.

We sat and talked for a while after we had finished eating and when we went outside I thanked them and headed west toward El Paso. I had a friend in El Paso, so this was a good chance to visit him.

My friend's name was Johnny Martinez and he lived in the Third Ward at the corner of Olive and Palm streets. This was the Mexican district of El Paso, and in those days the third ward was such a tough place that they couldn't even keep police out there to patrol the district. Johnny told me that they would send a tough cop or two out there and two or three days later they would find them dead in an alley or in an old empty house or shed. This was the El Paso of the early thirties. He took me out to see the Hole in the Wall, an island in the Rio Grande or Rio Bravo as the Mexicans call it. The real name of this place was Cordova Island, and it was the only neutral territory along the entire Mexican border.

This hole in the wall was where outlaws came back and forth across the river, and mainly the dope smugglers that were bringing heroin and morphine from Mexico to the United States. In Texas and Mexico and in fact most all of the southwestern United States at that time, marijuana, or griefo as the Mexicans called it, was more common than marigolds and sunflowers. It was a rare thing to find a Mexican along the frontera (border) that didn't smoke griefo at least now and then and most of them that I met used some of the weed daily.

I saw one Mexican die from using griefo. He got hooked so bad that he wouldn't eat, so consequently he starved to death in due time, in fact he didn't eat a bite of food for the last forty-two days he lived.

I tried a couple of those cigarettes at the insistence of some Mexican friends, but they didn't have any effect on me, thank the Lord, so I haven't touched one since. I don't see how anyone can get a bang out of such a thing. Maybe I'm just not normal. I know if a cow eats a bunch of that weed it goes crazy for a few hours. That is why the white ranchers in the west call it loco weed, loco means crazy in Spanish.

HERE AND THERE, OFF AND ON, NOW AND THEN

The railroad dicks arrested a couple of guys in the C.&E.I. yards at Danville, Illinois, and when they came before the city judge the dialogue became a joke that has no doubt been told many times, but the following are the true questions and answers at the trial.

The judge called the first man and asked, "What is your name?"

Answer, "Joe Smith."

Next question, "Is that the name your mother and dad gave you?"

Answer, "I don't know, I was just a baby."

Question, "Do you ever work?"

Answer, "Yes, now and then."

Question, "What do you do?"

Answer, "This and that."

Question, "Where do you do this work?"

Answer, "Here and there."

The judge said, "OK, wise guy, I'm going to send you to jail for ten days. Next."

The next man stepped up in front of the judge. Question, "What is your name?"

Answer, "John Brown."

Question, "Is that the name you use all the time?"

Answer, "Yes, nearly all the time."

Question, "Do you ever work?"

Answer, "Yes, now and then."

Question, "Where do you work?"

Answer, "Here and there."

Question, "What do you do?"

Answer, "I help him."

By this time the judge was pretty perturbed. He said, "Ten days for you two smart alecks and while you are doing your ten days you can help your buddy do his."

THE HOBO BED

Years ago every self-respecting professional hobo carried a roll of newspapers with him at all times. This was his bed. You can sleep on the ground in pretty cold weather if you will put down a few sections of paper to lie on and then cover yourself with a few more sections which you tuck under you as best you can, then put a section over your chest and face and tuck it under the back of your head so it won't fall off nor blow away.

There is a hard and fast rule of the road in regards to survival in cold weather. To wit: If you can keep your head warm, the rest of you will stay pretty warm. I knew and used this principle for years before I found out that it tells you this in biology books in the schools. It says that 60 percent of your body heat goes out through the top of your head.

This brings to mind a story that a great-aunt of mine told me many years ago. She lived next to a railroad and one morning after a big snow she looked out her back door and saw a mound of some kind in the snow by the railroad. She walked out to see what it was and saw the toes of a man's shoes just showing through the top of the snow.

She was sure she had found a dead man so she called the police. A big burly cop came out and raked the snow away from the bottom of one of the shoes and hit the shoe on the sole with his club. Instantly an old Irish hobo raised up and asked, "What the hell are you after doin mon, wakin me out of a sound sleep on a mornin like this?"

My aunt said, "When the old man raised up, newspapers flew all directions."

She said, "I felt guilty, so I took the old man in the house and gave him some hot coffee and fixed him a good hot breakfast."

SOUP BEAN ANNIE

parks, Nevada, used to be a division point on the Union Pacific Railroad. Sparks was three miles east of Reno. Knowing how this country has changed I am inclined to think that Sparks is probably part of Reno proper by now but nevertheless there is a story I think is worth telling about the Sparks of long ago. Not Sparks per se, but a lady who lived just north of the town of Sparks.

So I dedicate this to one of the unsung heroes of the not too distant past. It is the story of a lady who fed every hobo who came to her door and registered him or her, by name and address if any, in a big ledger that she kept just for this purpose. I first met her in the summer of 1932 and she had almost two ledgers of names at that time, and in certain cases the same name appeared several times over a period of years. These were her friends, the ones who came back to see her from time to time. At least she considered them as friends.

I have forgotten her real name but that wasn't important anyway, for we all called her Soup Bean Annie and that was the name she loved best. She was known by every professional hobo west of the Rockies, so in reality she was a national hero. A celebrity in her own right.

Annie lived a mile north of the U.P. yards in an old weather-beaten frame house in a grove of cottonwood trees. There was a pot of soup beans seasoned with bacon skin and two or three dozen biscuits always cooked and ready to eat at all times, and she actually enjoyed having "the boys" drop in for a bowl of beans and two or three biscuits. All she asked was that you visit awhile and tell her where you had been and where you were heading for now, and she was always concerned about how you had been getting along. I asked her why she did this and how she could afford to do it?

She said, "I have a little money and I can't think of a better way to spend it, as for why, it is sentiment. I married a wonderful man years ago and he had been on the road before I knew him, he tried to settle down but he just couldn't do it, so one day he left and I haven't seen him since. I pray every day that some day he too will drop in for a bowl of beans and a couple of biscuits."

THE MONSTER
OF OCONTO COUNTY

I used to go up into Wisconsin and Minnesota in summer and work in the harvest fields and that was some real fine country if you were looking for a few days' work, where the food was excellent and the pay good. I used to go through Chicago to where I could catch a North Shore electric train and ride out to Kenilworth, Winnetka, or Highland Park, then I would catch a northbound train on the Northwestern Railroad and I was on my way.

If it was early summer you could always find a job picking cherries in the Green Bay area and out on the peninsula in the Sturgeon Bay area or most anywhere as that entire peninsula is known as Cherry Land.

One summer when I was leisurely making my way to the grain fields, I was walking along the railroad in Oconto County, Wisconsin, and the day was hot, so I began looking for a creek or a small lake where I could take a dip and get cooled off and rest awhile.

I finally came to a little creek about eight feet wide and so clear you could see every pebble and grain of sand on the bottom, and that is remarkable even if the water is only ten or twelve inches deep.

I decided that since this little creek was so nice and the natural beauty of the place so appealing, I would stay here a day or two and just enjoy the scenery.

Moreover, this would be an ideal place to wash my clothes, bathe and shave and leave here looking like a gentleman. I had mooched a little sack of groceries, or as they say on the road dinged a lump, in the little town of Green Valley, so I had enough food to hold out for a day or two and besides there is always a lot of nutritious wild food around a place like this if you took the time to look for it, that is if you knew what it looked like to begin with.

As I stood there thinking how beautiful the creek and surrounding area was, it occurred to me that I could even do some fishing while I was here, for I had a line and several hooks and small sinkers and a little cork in a salve box in my bundle.

The fishing gear in that little tin box had fed me many times when dinging was bad or impossible in some remote section of the country.

I finally got undressed and took a washcloth and soap and went out to the center of the stream and washed my head and took a bath and decided to shave.

I had a little mirror with a wire handle on it, so I cut a stick and sharpened it on one end, went to the center of the stream and stuck the stick into the sandy bottom and hung the mirror on it, then I got my razor and soap and went into the creek and sat down in the water and started shaving.

When I turned my head so I could see in the mirror to shave the right side of my face I looked straight at the biggest water moccasin that I have ever seen. It was about four feet long and as big around as a quart bean can, or perhaps four inches in diameter at the largest part to be more specific. The snake was lying on a shelflike ledge of hard clay that ran along the bank of the creek, about six inches under the water. The snake didn't offer to bother me, but the sight of such a creature so close to me was more than I could conveniently bear, so I grabbed my little mirror and made a wild leap from the center of the creek to almost the top of the creek bank.

If I could have made such a standing broad jump when I was in school, I would have been a star.

After awhile I slipped down to the edge of the water to see if the snake was still there, but he was gone. I looked all around that area but I never saw him or it again.

With fear in my heart I went back into the water and finished shaving, then I washed my clothes and hung them on bushes to dry.

This episode just about took all the enjoyment out of this place, so I made up my bundle and when my clothes were dry I dressed and left after bathing.

MY LIFE AS A GYPSY

I was jungled up one time under a railroad bridge or viaduct and living like a king when suddenly a bunch of
gypsies showed up and taught me a new way of life, the
life of the "Mourning Pedlar." These people could empha-
size sad stories and hardships as no hobo had ever been
able to do.

The old lady was the head of the clan, but the old man
was the final authority in all things, and though he never
lifted a finger to do anything the reverence and service to
him was complete. The old folks had a thirty-year-old son
who had never lifted anything heavier than a bag of Bull
Durham. His wife spent all her time waiting on the men, in
fact she was on call twenty-four hours a day. This daughter-
in-law was such a frail but uncomplaining little person you
had to feel sorry for her, though in reality the men were
kind to her always. I never heard any of them argue nor
utter an unkind word to each other.

About the second day they were there the old lady asked
me, "Why don't you travel with us and be one of the family,
you could drive the car for me and that would help all of us."

I told her that I would take a shot at it, for a while at least,
so I became a gypsy of sorts. The next morning we went out
and she directed me to go to a little town. When we got there
she said, "Turn here and go up that alley and stop behind
that yellow house, the one that is fastened onto the back of
that store."

I pulled the car up there and stopped. She got out and
said, "You stay in the car and watch that back window and
when you see me wave my hand you come to the back door
and I'll have something for you."

She went to the back door and a middle-aged lady let her
in, so I waited.

About fifteen minutes later she came to the window and waved and I went to the back door. She handed me a case of canned kidney beans and said, "Put these in the car, Diddyki."

She later told me that Diddyki meant lookout in gypsy language. Before long she waved again and I went to the door and she gave me a peck of potatoes and a side of bacon.

Shortly after that I saw a man put her out the back door and shout, "I've told you for the last time you damned gypsies get out and stay out. The next time I catch you around here I'll put you in jail for a while."

She came to the car and said, "Let's go, Diddyki, before he finds out about this stuff and comes after us with a shotgun."

As we drove along she told me that the lady had also given her eleven dollars in cash, so she had done pretty good for about thirty-five or forty minutes, fortune telling.

She said, "That lady is nice, and she has a lot of faith in my readings, so she has always paid me well for my services."

Once when we were camped on the outskirts of my hometown the old lady decided she would walk into town and see if she could drum up a little business, so I stayed in camp that day.

She came back in the afternoon and had two dollars and fifty cents in money and a new suitcase that she said some lady had given her for making a reading.

A day or two later I decided that I would go visit my mother. We talked about things in general for a while and I told her that I was traveling with some gypsies and they were very kind, friendly people.

"I am just simply sick," she said. "A couple of days ago some real nice gypsy woman came here and wanted to give me a reading, so I invited her in. She tried to tell my fortune and was having some difficulty getting through, so she finally told me that I had been having some family problems lately and that I had set up a mental block that she couldn't get through.

"She said, 'Honey, if you have something new that you have handled recently, that you will let me take home and keep until tomorrow it will break the mental block and when I bring it back, I will be able to give you a good reading.'

"I gave her my new suitcase, but she never came back the next day, as she had promised."

I had to laugh and she asked me what I was laughing about?

I said, "I know where your suitcase is, Mom, and I will get it back for you."

When I got back to camp I told the old lady that she had clipped my mother for that suitcase, and she was sorry and said if she had known who the lady was, she wouldn't have taken the suitcase.

She said, "Your mother is kind, she also gave me fifty cents for my trouble. Now you can take the suitcase back to her and tell her I apologize."

When I took the suitcase home I told my mother to not trust people so readily or she might lose everything she had.

I told her, "Mom, if it wasn't for you Scotch-Irish and the Irish and Pennsylvania Dutch people, the gypsies would starve to death."

In Lancaster County, Pennsylvania, and all the Pennsylvania Dutch country you will find some of the most beautiful hex signs (good luck signs) painted on the front of many barns where it is visible from the road, and this is no doubt the most beautiful superstition in the world. Imagine what a life I have lived being a mixture of Pennsylvania Dutch, Scotch-Irish, Welsh, Irish and Delaware Indian. All of these people consider superstition an integral part of their daily lives.

THE JUNGLE BENEFACTOR
AT ST. JOE

One time I did a noble thing accidently. My buddy and I went into St. Joseph (St. Joe), Missouri, on the Wabash Railroad and as usual after a long ride we were hungry. We went uptown to work the stem and I agreed to get some meat and he was to get vegetables and bread so we could cook us a big can of Mulligan stew. Every place I stopped and dinged the proprietor would give me a big chunk of boiling beef about the size of a man's head, so I kept going in the anticipation of getting a little pork of some kind, for Mulligan is better if it has a little pork in it.

I wound up with about thirty pounds of boiling beef by the time we were ready to head for the jungle, and he had half a gunnysack of vegetables and bread.

We got out to the jungle and found about forty or fifty hoboes there, and some of them were complaining about this town being a hard place to get anything to eat. I couldn't agree with that, for we had found it to be one of the best places we had ever seen. I told my buddy that we would pick out what meat, vegetables, and bread we would need, and that I thought it would be nice if we gave all the rest of this grub to these guys, as there was enough to feed every bo in that jungle.

This is what we did and before long there were three or four big cans of Mulligan stew boiling here and there over the entire length of the jungle and everyone was happy, and I believe my buddy and I were the happiest of all, for there is a lot of truth in those old words, "It is better to give than it is to receive."

BETWEEN A ROCK
AND A HARD PLACE

Jack Ross and I were heading for a job that we had heard about, a job for a farmer, planting tomatoes. We were walking down a little railroad in southeastern Indiana and a storm was coming up and black clouds were rolling and lightning and thunder was flashing and booming on all sides. I kept watching the western sky for I had a feeling that this was going to be worse than just a bad storm. Finally I saw a greenish-black cloud down low and rolling, and there was a long black tail hanging from it and the tail was touching the ground.

I showed it to Jack and he said, "Hell, Chief, let's find a bridge and get under it."

We started running along the railroad and soon came to a big culvert. The culvert under the railroad was a four-foot steel tube anchored in a concrete abutment at each end. The entire culvert was perhaps fourteen feet long. We would be safe from the tornado in there, so in we went.

When we went in the culvert was as dry as a powder mill, so we knew it was one of those wet weather deals, designed to carry off excess rainwater during storms, and this can be dangerous, for these culverts are the flash flood specials.

We sat in there as the tornado passed over and thanked the Lord that we had found this culvert when we did.

After the tornado had passed the rain came down in sheets of water so dense you couldn't see over six feet beyond the ends of the culvert.

Then we heard a roaring sound that kept getting louder and we thought it must be another tornado coming, then we realized what it was. There was a wall of water coming down that ditch, and the water was four or five feet deep. We ran for the other end of the culvert and just barely got out of there in time. In fact as we were climbing up the bank onto the railroad right-of-way the water caught us and we were instantly soaking wet up to our knees. It was still raining hard but it was better to be wet than drowned.

About a mile down the track we came to a little town that had been badly torn up and the roof was gone off the elevator and an empty boxcar was lying on its side near the right-of-way fence.

Since we were already wet we started checking to see if anyone was badly hurt or killed, and fortunately only one man had gotten hurt badly enough to require a doctor. The man had been hit on the head with a piece of two-by-four that was flying through the air during the tornado. When the storm was over we asked for directions to the farm of our future employer and got out there without any further trouble.

The tornado had missed these people's house and barns by about half a mile, but even though they hadn't been hit, they were still scared about half out of their wits when Jack and I got there.

THE BURNING BOXCAR

I used to hobo around with a French and Indian guy about my age, and he was a character. He could imitate anything, animals, birds, frogs, almost any musical instrument, and anyone's talk and mannerisms, and he was a tramp, but today he (Bill Duvall) could have been a millionaire with even half the talent he had.

Once when Bill and I were caught in one of those subzero periods in midwinter in the North, we almost froze to death and at the same time came very close to destroying a lot of railroad rolling stock, as they call boxcars etc.

We got up into an empty boxcar about dark and rolled up in some heavy wrapping paper and went to sleep.

About 2:00 A.M. I awoke and was so cold I could hardly move or even talk. I called Bill and he too was awake but hadn't said anything. I told him that we had to get a fire going soon or we would freeze to death.

I said, "Let's go out and find some big rocks or bricks and a piece of tin and some wood or coal and start a fire up here in this car."

We hunted around for a few minutes and found a piece of sheet metal and some rocks, but no wood nor coal.

I told him to stay in the car and I would get something to make a fire. I raised up a boxing lid on the car and got a handful of oil-soaked waste and handed it to Bill and told him to tear it in half and lay half of it on the tin and light it and save the other half for later. Then I went around and got a handful of waste out of each box and put it up in the car. I was careful not to take too much and cause a hot box on that car that would or might burn up a journal (axle) later.

I got up in the car and was standing over the fire absorbing some much-needed heat when all of a sudden Bill said, "I'll get this damned place warm."

Before I realized what he was going to do, he threw that whole gob of waste on the fire and it lit up like it was soaked with gasoline.

Within ten seconds the entire car was full of fire and we had to jump out of there at once or be burned up. I had tried to kick the burning waste out the door, but that just spread the flames and made it worse. When we got about thirty feet from the car I looked back and the car looked like a huge torch.

I said a lot of mean nasty things to Bill, for in all my years on the road I had never caused a fire nor destroyed anything.

Fortunately this car was sitting out to itself and didn't ignite any of the others that were sitting about a block down the track. We didn't go back to check on it, but I am sure the car must have been completely destroyed. We went about a mile north of the railroad and found a gravel pit where there was a lot of wood to burn, so I got down behind a gravel bank and started another fire. We soon got warmed up and made it through the night.

The next morning I told Bill that I would go as far as his sister's with him and he could stay there or stay somewhere, but he wasn't going to travel with me anymore, and that's the way it was. Our days on the road as buddies were over.

WE'RE ALL THE WAY FROM TERRE HAUTE

I was living in Terre Haute, Indiana, in 1940 and that town was deader than last year's horse weeds, so I decided to go to Michigan and see if I could find a job.

While I was getting ready to go, a fellow that I knew slightly came along and when I told him where I was going he immediately wanted to go with me. He said that he was laid off from the steel mill where he had worked for several years.

I knew that he was playing with a short deck, as the saying goes, meaning that he was slightly nutty, but I told him that he was welcome to go if he was willing to accept life just as it was dealt out to us. He said he had always wanted to take a hobo trip just to see what it was like.

I told him to go home and pack a small suitcase with a few shirts, a couple pairs of pants, socks, underwear, handkerchiefs, shaving equipment etc. He was back within an hour and raring to go.

When we left my mother-in-law told me to take care of him and see that he didn't get hurt or killed.

As we were walking along the street I was thinking. I couldn't catch a freight train with this ding-a-ling, for he would be almost sure to get hurt or killed, so I decided that we would hitchhike.

When we got to the Terre Haute city limit I flagged a guy down and he took us about twelve miles up the road, and about every three minutes my companion would say, "We're going all the way to Michigan." This man we were riding with gave him some strange looks, for he must have realized that my hobo buddy was a "psychophonic compasinator," that's a dingbat that is going someplace and can't believe it.

This man let us out and we thanked him and soon got another ride. Just as soon as we got in the car my buddy said, "We're all the way from Terre Haute and goin all the way to Michigan." I didn't know whether to laugh or put him out of his misery. Everyone that gave us a ride were soon looking at us as though they thought we were a couple of fugitives from some nuthouse.

To keep from getting put out of every car, I had to keep explaining that this was his first trip on the road and he was spellbound by the novelty of it all.

When we were walking through towns he would holler at everyone that looked at him, "We're all the way from Terre Haute."

I tried to quiet him down, but to no avail. He just kept bugging his eyes out and hollering, "We're all the way from Terre Haute."

We finally got to Benton Harbor and I took him down to a factory where I had worked some years before. I talked to the personnel man and he said, "I think I can use both of you."

We went in to get a physical and he wouldn't drop his pants to get a hernia check. The doctor told him, "Don't worry, I always kiss a guy while I am feeling around."

This was the wrong thing to say. My buddy ran out into the parking lot and hid and it took me about ten minutes to find him.

I told him to come on back in and take the examination so we could get the job. He said, "No sir, I just knew he was one of those kind of guys when I looked at him. I'm going back to Terre Haute."

He couldn't have found his way back home so the only alternative I had was to escort him back to Terre Haute.

We left Benton Harbor and started walking south on U.S. 12. We got a couple of short rides and by the time we got to New Buffalo, Michigan it was getting dark so I started looking for a place to spend the night.

Before long we came to a large lighted sign on the west

side of the road, so we went behind it and found a nice grassy place to lie down and turned in for the night, or so I thought, but I soon found out that my bug-eyed buddy still wasn't ready to settle down.

There was a big lakeside hotel and health spa about half a mile northwest of us and the hundreds of lighted windows were visible through the trees.

My buddy asked, "What is that big building over there?" I told him it was an insane asylum, and that was the wrong thing to do, for he got scared and wanted to leave there immediately, so I had to do some tall persuading to get him to lie down and try to go to sleep.

There was a patch of swampy land between us and the lake (Lake Michigan) and as luck would have it there was a loon living or feeding in the shallow water of that swamp. My buddy had just started to doze off when that loon let out one of those blood-curdling screams that they are so famous for. He jumped three feet off the ground and said, "My God, what's that awful noise?" I told him that it was a loon.

He said, "You're kidding me, that's one of those crazy people that's gotten loose and is running around in that woods screaming."

He wouldn't accept an explanation, so I poured it on strong. I gave him just what he wanted to hear. I said, "Yes, the way it sounds there must be two of them."

He wouldn't take his eyes off that swamp, so he didn't sleep a wink all night. I laid down and went to sleep and when it was just starting to turn gray at the beginning of dawn he let a yelp out of him, grabbed his suitcase and ran out to the highway.

He had just gotten to the roadside when a car pulled up and stopped. It was a Michigan state trooper. The trooper asked, "What is the matter?"

My buddy started telling him about that big insane asylum and the woods being full of crazy people screaming all night.

You could tell the trooper got suspicious of my buddy's

sanity, for he asked, "Where are you from and what are you doing here at this time of the night?"

Old Bud started his chant. "We're all the way from Terre Haute, looking for a job, now we're all the way from Benton Harbor [about twenty miles] and going all the way back to Terre Haute."

I told the trooper that old scary Bud was with me and that this was his first time away from home and he was all shook up. Thank God those Michigan state troopers are nice people. Most lawmen would have put us in jail for observation, for they would have thought we were both nuts.

At this point I saw what had scared him when he ran out from behind that sign board yelling, "They're coming, they're coming."

Yes, they were coming all right. There was a cow grazing about seventy-five feet back of the sign board, it was no doubt some farmer's cow that had gotten out during the night.

The trooper said, "You fellows can ride with me down to the state line and that will help you a little." Then he told me, "You should get him home as soon as you can. I can see that he isn't cut out for this kind of life."

He winked at me and I said, "OK, officer, I'll get him home as soon as I can."

The tales he told when we got back to Terre Haute would have made a few real good horror movies. From that time on, when I was in Terre Haute and would see him I would rib him about taking another trip and he would actually run away from me shouting, "No sir! No sir! I still dream about those crazy people trying to get us that night."

THE TARANTULAS OF TEXAS

One time when I was down in Texas on a hitchhiking trip I stopped in a little town and dinged a grocery store operator out of some minced ham and a little five-cent loaf of bread and a bottle of water, then I walked west on the highway for about two miles until I came to a cement culvert, so I sat down and started fixing a sandwich. While I was doing this I noticed a large number of big black spiders coming across the road and my first impulse was to run, then I saw they were not really coming toward me but rather on a course that would take them about three or four feet to my right.

They passed me and went around the end of the cement and down the little bank and into the steel tube that ran under the road. They were tarantulas, or as they call them in the Southwest "hairy tarrantlers."

They came in a steady stream across the road, down the bank, through the tube and back across the road endlessly. There were perhaps five thousand dead ones mashed on the pavement where cars had run over them.

This was one of the most unusual things I have ever seen and I was watching them and eating and so absorbed that I didn't hear a car pull up and stop. The first thing I heard was when the man slammed the door shut when he got out. I looked up and there was a big Texas Ranger heading my way.

He came over and said, "Howdy, what are you doing?"

I told him I was eating and watching these spiders. Then he asked, "Are you on the road?"

I said, "Yes, sir, I am."

He said, "Get moving, we don't want no damned tramps

around here." Then as an afterthought he said, "It's nine miles to the county line, to the west, and if I see you stopped again I'll put you in jail, so just keep walking."

This was one man's idea of Texas hospitality in the 1930s. Thank God they were not all like that. Most of them were fairly decent humans.

THE FIRST VEGETARIAN
I EVER MET

As I have often said, "The road is a constant source of knowledge to those who have an open mind." The following story is a good illustration of what I am talking about.

On one of my leisurely sojourns through the San Fernando Valley in California I met a man that I will never forget and one that changed the whole pattern of my life and thinking to a large degree.

The train I was on went in the hole, pulled off on a siding to let a passenger train pass. The first thing I noticed was the vineyards, for there were ripening grapes as far as the eye could see in all directions.

I decided to look around, so I let the train go on north without me. I was strolling along the track marveling at the different kinds of grapes that were growing along the sides of the railroad right-of-way when I saw a man sitting in the shade of a little tree on the east side of the railroad. We spoke to each other and he invited me to come over and sit down and talk awhile.

I accepted his invitation and we sat and talked for perhaps half an hour about things in general, then he began to tell me about himself.

He was from San Diego and said that he had worked hard all his life and bought a nice home and had managed to save a little money, then just about the time he and his wife were getting things set up so they could kind of enjoy life, she took sick and died. They only had one child, a daughter, who was married and had a husband and two children. He said that he couldn't adjust to the life of a widower with a big seven-room house to take care of and he wouldn't marry again, so he gave the house, furniture and all, to his daughter and son-in-law and went on the road.

He said his wife had been dead for thirteen years and in all this time he had never slept in a bed nor ate any cooked meals. In my ignorance of a better way of life I began to feel sorry for him and told him so.

He smiled and said, "I guess you don't understand what I am talking about."

I said, "Perhaps not, but I think it is terrible that your daughter and her husband won't let you stay with them in your own home, where you could sleep in a bed and eat good home-cooked meals."

He said, "You are missing the point. I chose this way of life for health reasons and it's working."

He said, "For twelve and a half years I haven't known what it was to be sick or have an ache nor a pain like most people my age are subject to." He said, "Sleeping on the ground and eating only fresh raw food is the secret to good health."

He told me that he didn't eat meat of any kind and had found a diet of fresh fruits and vegetables to be much more satisfying and healthful than the conventional diet.

Then as is typical of most ordinary people I began to think he must be some kind of a nut.

He said, "I am sixty-eight years old. How old are you?"

I told him I was nineteen, and he said, "OK, let's see you do this."

He sat down on the ground and crossed his legs Indian fashion, extended his arms straight out on either side of his body, then rose to his feet without any apparent effort.

I tried to do what he had just done so easily, and finally after considerable effort I managed to get to my feet. I was embarrassed by having a sixty-eight-year-old man make me look so helpless and inept.

I began to notice that his complexion and movements were symbols of only one thing, perfect health.

He asked, "Why don't you stick around with me for a

while, if you aren't in any special hurry, and I'll teach you a few things about living right."

I agreed to stay with him for a few days and experiment with his way of life. The conventional human diet is almost identical to the conventional habit of smoking cigarettes, it is mostly fantasy.

I've heard many say, "If I don't have meat at every meal or at least once or twice a day I would starve to death." Others say they couldn't go to sleep at night if they didn't eat a big dish of ice cream about an hour before retiring. Others say, "If I had to give up cigarettes they might just as well shoot me." Or "I can give up anything but my cigarettes."

This is all pure fantasy. I was raised by meat eaters and cigarette smokers and drunks, so I know whereof I speak. You can live without anything that is not natural nor essential to human survival and live a lot better.

My friend and I spent most of the afternoon talking about the actual plan of the Creator as it applies to all living creatures. This man was very intelligent and extremely well versed in the field of diet and nutrition. I was amazed and pleased by the emphasis he put on what is natural and what is unnatural to not only man but to all creatures the Lord created. He was the first to point out to me that each species of creatures is governed by a plan and a natural law in regards to survival that mark each species as distinct individuals. He was also the first to tell me that all of the most intelligent creatures in the world are vegetarians, and that all things that actually serve man to any notable degree are vegetarians, with the exception of the dog, who is an omnivorous animal.

This was food for thought, so I tried to make a mental note of all that he said, and not once did I have an urge to doubt or question him on any point.

In those days the majority of ranchers in California wouldn't say anything to you for getting a handful of fruit or vegetables or a bunch of grapes to eat, so my friend and I eventually went into a vineyard and got a couple of bunches and came back to the railroad and sat down on a rail and ate supper.

For about the first two days I had a craving for all the junk food that I had been accustomed to eating, but since this craving was in my mind only, I soon got over it and really started enjoying my fruit diet.

I understand that the fruit ranchers on the West Coast nowadays will have you arrested if you even look like you are going to get a peach or a bunch of grapes or whatever.

It is logical to assume that many of the ranchers of my day had never read a Bible nor been inside a church, but they followed the Word to the letter, for it says in the Bible, "If you need anything, go into thy neighbor's field and get it, but do not take anything to waste nor anything to sell."

This part of the Christian doctrine is unknown to the Christians of today and to the ranchers of California and everywhere else. It used to be pretty much the same way in Florida, but a friend recently told me that it is virtually a crime to get caught taking anything out of those fruit groves down there.

It doesn't make much judicial sense to turn all types of violent criminals loose and put a person in jail for taking an orange or some other type of food when they are hungry.

My friend and I moved on down the railroad a couple of miles the next day and decided to spend a day or two by a vineyard where the vines were loaded with the largest grapes I had ever seen.

Time has dimmed my memory, but I am sure my friend told me these large grapes were some type of special wine grape. They were such a dark blue they appeared to be black from a distance of five or six feet. Regardless of what they were, they were pretty good food. I stayed with this man for two weeks and during this entire time all we ate was fresh fruit of one kind or another.

I soon reached the point of not needing nearly as much food as I had been led to believe a human needed to maintain good health and normal strength. Before long a medium-sized bunch of grapes or a couple of medium-sized peaches or apricots was enough to satisfy my hunger for four or five hours. You are getting pretty close to being right with nature when a minimum of food will give you complete satisfaction and do you more good than five times that amount has been doing.

Within the first four or five days I began to feel better and function better in every way and I was amazed by the fact that just a change of diet could make so much difference. I didn't know much about diet and nutrition at that time, but I got hold of a book a few years later that said it all, *You Are What You Eat* by Dr. Lindlahr. There could be no more truthful way to say it than is submitted by this simple title.

I enjoyed my few days with this man and I was most grateful for all the things he taught me. If I were to write a story about the most unusual man I ever met it would have to be this man. As the kids say nowadays, "He had it all together."

He kept himself neat and clean at all times and he explained how he did it. He wore gray whipcord pants and shirts and a gray felt hat and black work shoes and he explained that he had four of these whipcord uniforms, a dozen pairs of socks, and a dozen changes of underwear, shorts, and sleeveless undershirts.

He had half of this stuff in a laundry all the time and when the half he was using began to get dirty he would hop a freight and go to the town where the laundry was and pick up his clean clothes, go somewhere and bathe and put on clean clothes and leave the dirty clothes to be laundered and he would be back every two weeks to get his clean clothes and leave his dirty ones.

By using this system he managed to keep clean and presentable at all times, and like many people on the road he bathed every day if he happened to find a fairly secluded creek or pond.

This was a fine system, but I wondered how anyone on the road could afford all this laundry work. When I mentioned this to him he said, "I am on the road, but I'm not a tramp in the strictest sense of the word, for I have money in the bank in San Diego and I usually carry four or five dollars on me to pay for such things as laundry and any little services that I might need."

I have often thought what an ideal system of living this man had devised. He had the freedom of a hobo, but with an almost total lack of responsibility, the wisdom to employ a diet that is conducive to good health and all his food was free for the taking. He had money to buy what nature did not provide and he also had the great wisdom to know that there is a vast difference between the actual needs of humanity and the assumed wants.

I have often wondered what ever became of this unusual man. I know that he must have passed on, perhaps many years ago, but through the pen of this writer his philosophy will live for many years to come.

This was the first vegetarian I ever met and this was about as much of a shock as meeting a cab driver or a plumber from Mars. He carried a well-used Bible with him and delighted in quoting verses from his King James Bible to substantiate his claim that humans were created as vegetarians, and according to the Bible he was 100 percent right.

He read and showed me several places in the Bible that made it quite clear that man or humans are not supposed to eat meat or flesh. The word meat in the Bible does not refer to flesh but to fruits and vegetables. A good place to start is at the front of the Bible. Read Genesis 1:29, 30 for it is in these verses that the Lord tells the newly created humans what food they are supposed to eat. He showed me what it says in the Book of Isaiah 65:21, 22, 23, 24, and 25. These verses make it clear that before there can be any peace in the world all things must become vegetarians. Isaiah 66:3 and 4 make it pretty obvious that flesh was not meant to be a food.

This man was also the first person in my lifetime to make

me aware of the power of the sun and the leading part it plays in the overall scheme of things in the entire universe.

He laid it on me straight when he asked, "What would happen if the sun did not shine for six consecutive months?"

I said, "I imagine everything in the world would die."

Then he asked, "What do you think would be here now, if the sun had never shined?"

I said, "It's pretty obvious that without the sun, there would have been nothing!"

He said, "You are right. The sun is the sole creative power of the universe."

I said, "Yes, this appears to be the real truth, for everything you have said is self-evident."

There is a saying, "You will see or hear anything imaginable in California if you will stay there long enough."

There are many things that are based on theory and pure fanaticism, and these I would never accept. The truth of all things I will accept, so long as it is tangible and provable. Any genuine truth that affects humanity or all life of any kind must of necessity be provable and tangible.

Anything that you cannot prove by reasonable means and logic is purely theoretical fantasy.

This man from San Diego taught me how to distinguish truth from fantasy, in fact it is my belief that he taught me more in two weeks than I had learned in the nineteen years before I met him.

After I left this man and resumed my journey back to Indiana all went well until I left Sacramento and headed east over the hump to Reno.

GREEN BAY JACK

I was walking down the old U.P.
With my bindle on my back
When I met a bo I used to know
Known as Green Bay Jack.

We talked of places we had been
And of things we'd said and done.
We talked of jungles and water tanks
And the times we'd had to run.

We built a fire and fixed some grub
And talked till almost dawn.
We'd catch a nap and rise with the sun,
For we'd soon be moving on.

DEATH IN THE LUMBER CAR

While I was in the U.P. yards at Sacramento I met a young Jew from St. Louis. He was going home so since I was going through St. Louis anyway we decided to buddy up and travel together. When we got almost to the top of the Sierra Nevada mountains on the hump it started getting cold and the higher we went the colder it got. Neither of us were dressed for winter weather so we nearly froze.

This was a redball freight so all the cars were loaded and sealed and there was no choice but to ride the tops.

There was one low-side gondola about midway of the train, and it was loaded with lumber, so we decided to ride it. That would be warmer than sitting on top of a boxcar. Just before we reached the summit my buddy got so cold he decided to get down in the space between the front end of the car and the lumber and lie on the floor of the car.

I tried to persuade him not to do it, but to no avail. I looked down on him about half an hour later and he was lying down there with his coat up over his head, sound asleep. There was a full moon and a billion stars out that night, so it was almost as light as day.

This was in mid-August but the summit was covered with deep snow and as the train went through a cut in the pass I could see a bunch of those bighorn mountain goats or sheep standing on the cliff high above us, looking down on the train as it passed by. This was quite a sight, but I was too cold to really enjoy it. As we started down the eastern slope I tried to awaken my buddy and make him get out of there and get up on top of the lumber with me, but he assured me that he was safe and warm down there and he was going to stay where he was until we got to Reno.

I said, "If that engineer should apply the brakes hard and

quick it could cause this lumber to shift and mash you against the end of the car."

He said, "It can't shift, it is tied down solid with steel bands, you are just overly cautious. Wake me up when we get to Reno."

I had did all I could, so I pulled my coat up over my head and tried to keep from freezing as that fast freight rambled on down those steep mountain grades toward Reno.

We were perhaps halfway down the eastern slope when the engineer hit the brakes hard, and BOOM! that lumber hit the front end of the car so hard it sounded like a cannon. I went up there and called to my buddy and prayed that he would answer, but there was no answer, so I knew that he was gone. An experienced bo would never take such unnecessary chances, no matter how cold it was.

When the train pulled into Sparks, which was the division point three miles east of Reno, I climbed down onto the ground and found the brakeman and told him there was a dead man in that carload of lumber. I explained how it had happened, who he was, and where he was from.

As soon as the brakeman went to notify someone, I pulled a disappearing act for I had no desire to see what they were going to find when they moved that lumber. I knew that young Hebrew and I liked him, so I wanted to remember him as I knew him in life, but not as hamburger.

He had told me his dad had a little shoestore on Market Street in St. Louis, Missouri. I was acquainted with the area, as east Market Street was the skid row district of St. Louis in those days.

I found his dad's store without any problems. I walked in and was greeted by an old man. I asked him, "Are you Mr. X?"

He said, "Yes, what can I do for you?"

I came right to the point. I said, "I knew your son. We traveled together some on the road."

He asked, "You did? He is now dead, did you know that?"

I said, "Yes, I was with him when he got killed."

94

I explained in detail exactly how it happened and he was quite pleased to know that I had tried to save his life and that he had died so quickly and painlessly.

He said, "Thank God, if he must go, that was the best way."

He insisted I stay awhile and finally conned me into staying a week. The day finally came when I got afraid that I would get used to living like that and mess up a perfectly happy hobo's life, so I told the old man and his wife that I must be going.

When I was ready to go the old lady handed me a package of food wrapped in newspaper and the old man tried to hand me a twenty-dollar bill, but I refused to take it. He finally insisted that I take five dollars or they wouldn't let me leave. He stuck the five bucks in my shirt pocket, then he asked me to come back and see them any time.

I never got back to see them, but my sympathy was with them, for the young man that was killed in the lumber car was the only child they had.

FROM WINNIPEG TO THE WABASH

One time when I was working in the harvest fields of Wisconsin and we were about done with the harvesting and thrashing in that area a man I had been working with by the name of Charlie Groves told me that I could find plenty of work in Manitoba, Canada, if I wanted to go up there.

When we got through and I got my money I caught a freight and went into Minneapolis, Minnesota, and started hitchhiking north to the Canadian border.

I finally wound up in Winnipeg, Manitoba, and was told to go to an office and sign up and they would send me out on a job. I found the office, which was about the same thing as a U.S. employment office, and they sent me to a big grain farmer seventeen miles northwest of Winnipeg. I worked for this man about two weeks and when he was done he sent me to a friend of his who was needing a man. I got about ten days' work there, and since it was late summer and I had a pretty nice bankroll I decided to head south.

About a week later I wound up on the Wabash River at Terre Haute, Indiana.

I decided to build a shack and winter there. I bought a dozen big galvanized tin signs and some used two-by-fours and built a pretty nice little shack.

An old lady gave me a two-hole monkey stove (laundry stove) and before long I was housekeeping in a big way. I built a bunk, a table, and a couple of stools and made some wall cabinets out of some wooden boxes and I was set for winter.

I bought an old axe for fifty cents to cut wood for my stove, as there was all the wood along the river that anyone would ever need. So keeping warm wasn't much of a problem.

About the time it began to get real cold I ran out of money

to buy food, so I had to promote a deal that would feed me through the winter.

I went to a big wholesale fruit and vegetable warehouse and made arrangements with the boss to save some over-ripe or damaged fruit and vegetables, specked potatoes, and the like and I was to be there twice a week to get all the edible stuff they were going to throw away. This was some deal. I wound up feeding about twelve or fifteen families, for there was no way I could ever use all this food. As an example they gave me one hundred dozen overripe pink bananas one time, so I had to enlist the help of some of those men I was feeding, and we hauled bananas for half a day in a big pushcart and distributed them to all these needy families.

It was a treat to see those little half-starved kids eat those big pink bananas, many of the smaller ones, four or five years old, had never saw a banana in their lives, much less ate one.

I ate bananas until I was swelled up like a poisoned toad, as the saying goes. I always had enough fruit and vege-tables at my shack to feed forty or fifty people at all times.

Then of course there was the problem of providing bread and other bakery products to fill my needs, so I went to a big wholesale bakery and made arrangements to pick up the damaged and second-day bread and pastry and as pay for this I agreed to sweep the big processing room twice a week. This too turned out to be a landslide, for in no time at all it got out of hand and I was forced to get the men together to help me carry and haul the stuff away from the bakery.

They gave me from fifty to a hundred loaves of good bread every time I went over there, and cookies, rolls, donuts, bismarcks, and so on, by the big cardboard box full. I have gotten as many as ninety to one hundred of those one-pound spice cakes many times. After I got this going I was pretty well able to feed all these families what might be called a well-rounded diet, at least they were getting plenty to eat, such as it was.

The automatic bread slicer had just been invented at that

time and they used to tear up dozens of loaves of fresh hot bread every day. They would put these parts in big cardboard boxes and save them for me, so it was that I sometimes got torn up bread while it was still hot.

I had to promote some butter some way, so I went to a big creamery and asked if they had any damaged butter? The superintendent said, "Yes, we have butter to fall off the conveyor onto the floor and we just throw it away, in fact we throw a lot of stuff away that is about 98 percent good, such as ice cream and other products that we make here, for if it is damaged in any way we can't sell it." So I made arrangements to come over two or three times a week and pick this stuff up, if they would be kind enough to save it for me.

He promised that they would save everything that was fit to eat and keep it in the cooler until I came after it. Then he said, "We have so much waste here, so maybe you had better come three times a week."

I went over to the creamery one time and someone had upset a truck of chocolate ice cream bars, and they had seventy-eight boxes for me, a dozen bars in a box. My poor friends and I lived high on the hog for a few days.

I got all nearly empty syrup cans, with all the different kinds of syrup they put in ice cream, and believe me, this stuff is delicious.

This promoting of mine was a godsend to these twelve or fifteen families that were benefiting by it. This was one of the greatest periods of my life, for I was able to help people that needed help. I made a lot of friends and taught them the art of promoting honestly when you have no other way to go.

EATING RATTLESNAKE

I came into Cheyenne one time on the D.&R.G.W. (Denver and Rio Grande Western) from Denver and found the famous Cheyenne Roundup in full bloom. Cheyenne was a fairly small town at that time, but this big annual rodeo show practically turned it into a metropolis. People come from everywhere to participate in this roundup as performers, spectators, hustlers, chiselers, and you name it.

I got into the act in my own way. Being a hobo I hoped to be able to pick up a couple bucks and a meal by helping someone out with some of the usual rodeo chores.

This was in the early thirties and the Depression was just starting to bite pretty deep into people's pocketbooks, so I found it hard to get even an hour's work, and a day's work was out of the question, so I was just sight-seeing for the most part.

I eventually came upon an old Indian who was making horsehair lariats by twisting and plaiting the long hairs from the tails of horses. This was a fascinating thing to watch, so I stopped. The old man and I soon struck up a conversation and he told me, "This horsehair rope making is almost a lost art, for very few young Indians can do it nowadays."

We talked for a few minutes more and he said, "Here, take this dollar and go to a store and get some minced ham and a loaf of bread and we will eat." I found a store nearby, so I was back in a few minutes. We made sandwiches and while we were eating he told me his name and where he was from and I did the same.

He said, "I am a Blackfoot Indian from Browning, Montana, and my name is Jim Little Plume."

We had taken a liking to each other right from the start,

so I wasn't too surprised when he told me how to find his house and invited me to come and visit him any time.

I stayed with him nearly all afternoon and when I finally decided that it was time to go we shook hands and he said, "Remember, Charlie, you are always welcome, so come and see me."

While we were talking he mentioned that rattlesnake meat was his favorite meat, and I said, "Well, Jim, I've heard of people eating rattlesnakes, but that's not for me."

About two years later I came into Browning, Montana, one afternoon and decided to look him up.

He had said, "Charlie, come twenty miles straight south of Browning on that road and you will come to a big creek, and that log house on the west side of the road by the creek is where I live."

I hitchhiked down there from Browning without any trouble. The man that picked me up knew Jim, so he took me within fifty yards of Jim's house. I got out and thanked him and he went on.

Then I smelled the aroma of food cooking and it was so delightful that it made me hungry instantly. As I started to the house a black and white fox terrier ran out and was fixing to get himself a mess of my leg when Jim came to the door and called him. I was surprised to find that Jim remembered me, for without hesitation he said, "Hello, Charlie! Come on in, I'm just fixing supper and I've got enough for both of us. Guess I knew I was going to have company."

I asked, "What is that, Jim, that smells so good?"

He said, "Some wild meat, you wait and see if you like it."

That smell couldn't be wrong. I knew I would like it, and I did.

After we ate, he said, "You told me you wouldn't eat rattlesnake, but you seem to like it as well as I do."

It was delicious, but since it is about six or seven dollars a pound on the market, I haven't eaten any since.

I stayed a week with Jim and he took me all over that country and introduced me to half the Indians around there.

I went back to see him about three years later and he had died of tuberculosis several months before. I lost a good friend when that old Indian died, and good friends are hard to come by.

GOOD DAYS AND BAD
WITH HOBOES AND DO-GOODERS

Some of the most enjoyable days I have ever spent were when I was sitting around a campfire reminiscing with a few genuine road men friends of mine that I hadn't seen for a year or two.

Every real old-time hobo was a walking storybook that you could listen to for hours and never get tired of hearing them recount their experiences, and they were just as eager to listen to yours.

Even an amateur who had only been on the road a year or two could tell a multitude of interesting true stories that would even delight the hearts of the old-timers.

I used to meet those old-timers when I was a kid and the first impression I got of them was, these men had gained a thousand years of experience in sixty-five or seventy years on the road.

They were good men for the most part, but they were rough men when the need arose. We were all capable of getting rough if we had to, for you had to be rough to survive. There was always a bad element to deal with wherever you went, and none of them were real hoboes. They were yeggs, fugitive murderers, bloodthirsty brakemen and conductors, mean railroad detectives, and the petty larceny city police and town marshals who couldn't or didn't have guts enough to catch a criminal but they could and did give a poor inoffensive hobo hell every time they got a chance. These jaybirds were total misfits so they had to do something to earn their money, and a hobo was about the easiest pickings they could find.

Then there was always a certain percentage of "good citizens" who tried to abuse and take picks on every hobo they saw.

As an example, I will tell you about one of these do-gooders in Green River, Wyoming.

I got off a freight at Green River and walked uptown. They had a half-inch galvanized pipe sticking up about three feet above ground, with a fountain bowl on top of it. Many towns in the West had this type fountains in those days.

I saw a fountain in front of a garage and asked the proprietor if I could get a drink?

He said, "Yes, help yourself."

As I bent over to drink he yelled at me, "Hey, boy, are you a tramp?"

I said, "Yes, I am."

He said, "Get out of here, no damned tramp drinks from my fountain."

I said, "You SOB, I'll break you of that bad habit."

As I was saying this I jerked the top off the fountain and threw it straight at his head, but unfortunately it hit him in the middle of his chest. Even so it shook him up a little and he screamed for the town marshal.

A little old guy came running at me with a .45 six-shooter that was half as long as he was, yelling, "Halt!" The railroad was only a block from the garage so I took off in that direction. The train I came in on was ready to leave, so I planned to catch it and get out of there.

As I ran toward the railroad I heard the engineer pulling the slack out of the couplings, then he blew a high ball and by the time I reached the railroad the train was moving out nicely.

I grabbed a gondola and climbed aboard. I picked the gondola, as the marshal was threatening to shoot me, so I would let him shoot the steel sides of the car instead of me. I waved at him and said, "Good-bye, Dad, take care of yourself and I'll see you later." I couldn't hear what he was saying, but it wasn't nice, for he was waving his gun at me and raising hell.

This is just one example of some of the dirty characters the old-time hobo had to deal with.

When you walked into a jungle, most any hobo that had scored (got a lot of food) would invite you to eat with him and it was a sincerely friendly gesture. Now and then you met what they call a "Single-O-Dick Smith from Cincinnati," this was a guy that was all for himself and any self-respecting hobo had no use for such a character.

If I told you that the life of a hobo was all milk and honey or peaches and cream, I would be lying, for even the bank president's life isn't all roses, nor is anyone's, for that matter. It takes all kinds of people to make a world, and each and every one has his own problems that are all relative to your life as an individual and are more or less governed by your environment.

There are three things that determine what kind of a human you are or want to be and an absence of either one can ruin your whole life and destroy your image with mankind or all humanity.

The three most important things are faith, morals, and principles, without them you are lost.

Any normal human can be as good or as bad as they want to be, there is no formulas nor law, nor hard and fast rule that can determine and govern your destiny. You are what you want to be, regardless of where you are or what you are doing.

SANDHOUSE HOTEL

I don't imagine there are or were many of the old-time hoboes who haven't slept in a sandhouse at least a few times and perhaps many times if they were on the road very long.

The sandhouses were usually near a roundhouse, where all engines are inspected after each run. Then they were serviced and made ready for the next run. The water tank or tender was filled, the coal tender was loaded to capacity, and the dome type sandbox on top of the engine was filled. After an air and machinery inspection the engines were put on the outbound track and were ready to be put in service when needed.

Now back to the old sandhouse, as it relates to the hobo and the tramp and perhaps the bums sometimes.

These sandhouses were heated with live steam pipes to keep the sand dry at all times, and this made an ideal place to sleep on cold nights. I was in a sandhouse one cold winter night at Columbus, Ohio, at the Columbus roundhouse of the Pennsylvania Railroad, which was a division point where they change crews and sometimes both engines and crews.

I was sleeping the sleep of the innocent, when all of a sudden I was awakened by a movement of the very sand I was lying on. At first I couldn't imagine what was happening. Then it dawned on me that someone was filling a sandbox and I was lying directly over the sand pipe. I quickly moved to the back wall of the sandhouse and went back to sleep.

Here's a note of caution. Don't ever get caught asleep in a sandhouse when they are filling it! But of course this will be in daylight, so you wouldn't be in there anyway.

Sandhouses are specifically a nighttime accommodation and should be treated as such.

I can remember a thousand cold nights when I have enjoyed the warmth of a sandhouse and thanked the Lord for the privilege of sleeping in a good warm place while many thousands of people all over the country were half-frozen, even in homes, where there was no money to buy coal or any type of fuel.

It has been my experience that there are thousands of home guards that would be a lot better off on the bum. They would definitely have more and live better.

On a cold night when you crawled into a sandhouse you could usually find two or three bos up there ahead of you, and it was always like a family reunion when you met one or two that you had known for a number of years.

Sometimes when you met someone that you hadn't seen for two or three years you would lie there and talk until two or three o'clock in the morning, trying to catch up on what had happened and where.

Hoboes have a social life quite similar to human beings. The greatest place to fraternize is a good hobo jungle. I have seen many lifelong friendships born in the jungles, as well as several nutty disputes settled.

Fights in hobo jungles are usually as needless and as brutal as the senseless fights that occur in conventional society.

I once met an old widow woman when I was walking along the C.&E.I. south of Terre Haute, Indiana, from what she told me she didn't have any way of getting along and as a result she was about half-frozen most of the winter. I told her that I couldn't feed her, but I could see that she had plenty of coal to keep warm in winter.

I told her, I usually came by her house about every ten days to two weeks, and that I would throw a bunch of coal off as I was passing by.

She asked me, "Aren't you afraid that you will get into trouble if you steal coal for me?"

I said, "No, not in the least, you let me worry about that."

106

The old lady lived beside the C.&E.I. main line and there were branch lines leading off the main to a dozen big coal mines in that area, so coal wasn't really a problem except to an old lady who couldn't help herself.

I asked the old lady if she had a way to haul the coal home and she said, "Yes, I've got a coaster wagon that I haul stuff on." Since she lived only about two hundred feet from the railroad the little wagon would do the job nicely.

A few days later I was in Sullivan, Indiana, in what was then known as the Depot Town Hobo Jungle when a coal drag stopped nearby. A coal drag is a train that is made up of nothing but coal cars. I decided to catch that baby and throw off some coal for the old lady.

I picked out a big car of shoulder lump (large chunks) of block coal. When the train pulled out I got on that car and sat on the front bumper and rode until I was within a few miles of the old lady's home, then I climbed up on top of the car and began piling a row of big chunks along the west side of the car. I built the row as high as I could without it falling off of its own accord. As we came near the old lady's home I sat down on the coal in the car, close enough that my feet would reach the row of chunks that I had piled up, then I waited. As we passed by in front of the house I kicked the row of chunks off onto the ground. I imagine I kicked off perhaps a ton in about twenty to twenty-five seconds.

I continued this procedure from time to time until around the first of October, and one day I got off a slow-moving train near her house and walked up to see how much coal she had. She took me out to her coal shed and showed me. She had coal stacked in there up to the roof. I don't think she could have put another chunk in that shed.

She was as happy as a kid with a new toy. I told her, "Well, it looks like you will keep warm this winter." She said, "Yes, thanks to you, I will."

I said, "As long as we both live I will continue to throw you off some coal every year."

She lived about two years from when I met her and someone found her dead in bed. The coroner listed the cause of death as heart failure, so I am happy in the knowledge that I was able to make her last two years a little easier.

When you do a good deed for someone in need, it is like a tonic for the spirit of man.

The old Cherokee Indian lady that partly raised me was as poor as Job's turkey but she had a heart as big as a mountain. She did washings for a living so naturally she never had enough money to go around. I decided that the least I could do was to steal enough coal to keep her house warm during the winter, and that is what I did.

I was never a thief in the strict sense of the word, but I have stolen coal when I was cold and I would unhesitatingly do it again under the same circumstances and still not be a confirmed thief.

During my years on the road I always worked and paid my way when I could and I still think this is the best way to do it, but if I am denied this opportunity I will still live some way, for this world owes each and every one of us a living of some kind. Since you did not ask to come here in the first place, it is a mortal cinch that something or someone should guarantee you a living if you can't make it for yourself.

NOTES ON HOBO JUNGLES

The little town of Elsworth, Indiana, was later renamed Edwards and years later was renamed again. This time they called it North Terre Haute. There used to be a strictly modern hobo jungle about a mile north of town at what was known as Otter Creek Junction or by a more popular local name as Crabbs Switch.

You are probably wondering how could a hobo jungle be modern. The answer is: This little jungle had everything you needed to live comfortably. It was on the bank of a little creek, so you could wash your clothes and take baths and shave whenever you took the notion. There was a little grove of trees right by the creek, so you had a lot of good shade to sit or lie in on hot summer days and there was a woven wire line fence that ran alongside the railroad and this fence made an ideal clothesline to dry your clothes on. There was also a bridge over the creek with enough high and dry land under one end for a dozen men to jungle up very comfortably when the weather was bad.

The creek was in reality a small spring-fed stream and the water at that time was pure enough to drink, so water to cook with and drink was right at hand in great abundance.

The nearest house was a good half-mile from this little jungle, so there was ample privacy for even the most sensitive and discriminating hobo.

Thirty-five or forty years ago there were hobo jungles all over the country and they were like everything else that I have ever seen, for some were good, some were bad, and some just mediocre. I think the worst jungle I ever visited was one on the northern outskirts of Terre Haute along the Milwaukee Railroad. It was down in an old gravel pit, and it was appropriately called "Death Valley." There were no trees for shade and not even a bush to break the cold winter winds that howled through there from November to March. There was a large pond in the bottom of the pit that was literally full of fish, but they were not over three inches long, for they were so inbred that they had become a race of midgets.

Even a hobo won't waste any time catching three-inch fish, so these little fellows were perfectly safe.

There was a story years ago about some wise guy that walked into a jungle and said, "I'll give the laziest man here a five-dollar bill if he can prove that he deserves to win it."

Some guy who was lying on the ground resting and smoking a cigarette said, "Roll me over and put it in my pocket, will you buddy?" He won!

There were two pretty good jungles at Macksville, West Terre Haute, Indiana, on the main line of the old Pennsylvania Railroad. One was on the north side of the track, between the railroad and U.S. 40 highway, on the bank of Mackleroy's pond. There was plenty of wood and good water available at both of them.

Someone had dug holes about four feet deep about ten or twelve feet back from the edge of the lake and the edge of the pond that were three-fourths full of good clear water at all times, and it was fairly cool, enough so that it was pleasant to drink.

Both the pond and lake were full of fish of all kinds and all sizes. It was easy to catch catfish at Mackleroy's pond, so I had all the fresh fish I could eat when I was jungled up at that pond. As I mentioned earlier, I always carried the necessary fishing gear with me at all times, so I have fished all over the country and caught some good ones on occasion.

BIG FISH
AND SOAP BUBBLE PROSPERITY

The best fishing I ever did during my years on the road was done by hand in an irrigation ditch at Belen, New Mexico. I was camped in a little jungle in a grove of cottonwood trees by the east end of the Rio Grande River bridge. I noticed a big irrigation ditch that ran in a westerly direction from the river, so I decided to look it over.

I found that it was about six or eight feet wide at the bottom and the water was all the way from one inch to two feet deep. The deeper holes were well stocked with big fish. I took my shoes and socks off and rolled my pant legs as high as I could and waded into one end of a deep hole and drove the fish downstream into the shallow water. Once they got into water one or two inches deep I could catch them easily. I would simply run one down and grab it with my hands and put it far enough back on the bank that it couldn't get back into the water and go after another one. I had a lot of fun and caught several big fish. There were eight of us camped there and we had all the fish we could eat, not only for that day, but for every day for a full week. Then I decided it was time to go on, so I left.

About fifteen years later I took one of my brothers down there and I didn't know the place, they had changed the appearance of the Rio Grande, cut the cottonwood trees down, built a big new concrete bridge, and discontinued the big irrigation ditch and filled it in. I could see that I had been fortunate enough to have been there in much better days.

Modernization and progress will eventually destroy all the true values of our natural environment. In fifteen years Belen had changed from a typical little western town of eleven hundred people, wooden buildings and board sidewalks and dirt streets, to a city of forty thousand people, modern stone, brick and concrete houses and business buildings, concrete sidewalks and streets and even two or three big factories that were empty and not being used for anything.

I asked a man what the hell happened to Belen? He said, "Friend, you wouldn't believe it, but all this happened during World War Two. The government built defense plants here and at one time the population went up to eighty thousand people, most all of them connected with defense work in some way. When the war ended the factories laid everyone off and closed their doors.

"The people couldn't pay for those big fine modern houses, so they sold their furniture and left, in the hope of finding some place where they could make a living.

"When those government men came here the first thing they started talking about was rebuilding the whole town, new modern houses to attract a lot of new people to this part of the country to carry on the defense work, etc. But this was just a wild dream and a temporary thing.

"As soon as the war was over these people had no way of paying for all of this modernization, so as a result there are thousands of new empty houses all over this town and these big dream boys haven't the faintest idea what they are going to do with them. The only things that can live in the desert without lots of money are prospectors, coyotes, jackrabbits, sidewinders, and lizards."

We told the man good-bye and left. I told my brother, "Let's get out of here, this is even much worse than the worst towns in the North and East."

The new bridge across the Rio Grande is unique in the context that it is the only bridge in the country that has a Y in the middle of the bridge, where two big highways fork. One goes straight east and the other goes southeast.

Since the real Belen was gone forever, perhaps, I was indeed glad to be on my way again. Wartime prosperity and wild dreams are like a soap bubble in a high wind, they can't possibly last long. Thank God for that.

THE TURKEYS OF
KANAWHA RIVER "KA-KNOW-EE"

I was coming down the Kanawha River from Charleston to Point Pleasant, West Virginia, on the B.&O. (Baltimore and Ohio) branch line that hauls coal out of those mountains. It was a beautiful sunny spring morning, one of those rare days when the whole world seems to be just right.

I was sitting on an empty flatcar with my feet hanging over the side, dangling freely in the clean morning air, which is a no-no as far as professional hobo practice is concerned, for it is risky business to ride a train with your legs dangling out of a boxcar door or from the side of any kind of car. In reality this is almost as dangerous as catching the back end of a car on a moving train, or getting off the back end of a car when a train is moving. But, as I said, everything was all right and I was happy, so I let my hair down a little. The railroad ran alongside the river for several miles, perhaps seventy-five to a hundred feet apart, with a strip of woods along the riverbank. I began to hear an unusual sound of some kind and started trying to locate it. I first thought it was something on the train, maybe a hotbox or something dragging on a rail.

Then I noticed that every one of those trees along the river was full of wild turkeys and they were all talking at once. What a racket. I don't know why they were all assembled there, but it must have been some special occasion for there were thousands of turkeys in those trees for a distance of perhaps two or three miles.

I told a man from Point Pleasant about it, and he informed me that he had seen the same thing twice in his lifetime, but could give no reason for it.

THE LORD WAS WITH ME
THAT NIGHT

I have often heard the phrase, "The Lord was with me!" An experience I had years ago in eastern Utah taught me the true meaning of those words.

There is a railroad running east out of Ogden, Utah, and across the Rockies and Colorado. I'm not sure, but I think this was the Rock Island Railroad. Anyway, I was coming back East one time and landed in Ogden one afternoon. The word was that there was a train going east at 6:50 P.M. so I decided that this was my baby. I should eat breakfast in Denver in the morning. The Pollock (Alex Chachinshi) was my buddy, he and I had ridden many thousands of miles together and no better man ever crawled into a boxcar. At the last minute something just told me to lay over there that night. I told Alex that we should find us a place to sleep and get a good night's sleep and go on in the morning. He agreed, so we walked down through the yards and found us a watermelon car that had about a foot of clean straw in it. We dug in and had a good night's sleep, and about 7:30 A.M. we went downtown and the newsboys were yelling, "Extra, extra, read all about it!" The headline said, "Train Crew and 55 Hobos Die in Crash, Engine and First 15 Cars Fall 1000 Feet into Colorado River." Suspension bridge collapses.

This was all I had to know and I was heartbroken. The train that left Ogden at 6:50 P.M. was the one that ended up in the Colorado River.

I actually got down on my knees and thanked the Lord God for sparing me, for I usually rode about twelve to fifteen cars back of the engine.

I had talked to some of those guys the night before. I remember the guy who was buckling a belt around a small leather bag so that his worldly possessions would be safe. Safe for whom, God? I found it hard to believe, yet there it was. Friendly faces and good hearts, without names. Victims of a society that sponsors poverty and encourages hoboism. A society that thinks you are all right as long as you can pay them, but when they have to pay you, you are no good. Most of these men were job hunters, people who were victims of the Depression, but few indeed were really hoboes in the strict sense of the word.

Hoboing is a philosophy, a way of life that few can accept and cope with. The real hobo is purely and simply a wanderer at heart and enjoys this way of life. To work a few days and get a few bucks in his pocket to pay his way, then move on, is a hobo's idea of living in style.

Regimentation and the theory of assuming all kinds of unnecessary obligations as a way of life are to a real hobo the least desirable of all things.

An old bo told me in the Big 4 yards at East St. Louis, Illinois (Brooklyn Yards), quote, "A man can call me names and run me out of any place but when he tries to take my freedom away from me, I'll kill him."

So, freedom and peace of mind are the key issues in hobo philosophy. I have often thought how unusual it is that few real hoboes die with heart attacks and cancer.

CATCHING THE MANIFEST
AT NAPTOWN

I was down in the southwest corner of Indianapolis one afternoon in the jungle that had been set up along the south side of the Pennsy main line where the Belt Line comes around the south edge of Indianapolis and intersects with the main line. All the freight trains went around the Belt and the passenger trains went right through the center of the city to the depot, which was in the near uptown district. I was going west so I kept listening for something to come around the Belt.

I finally heard a train coming so I picked my pack up and got ready to go. I could tell by the sound of that short sharp exhaust that this gentleman was going somewhere in a hurry, and that was fine.

There were four or five black men sitting there and one of them said, "You ain't going to get that baby, buddy. That's a meat-a-fest [meaning manifest]."

I said, "Well, she will have to be going pretty fast if I don't get her when she goes onto the main."

All trains coming off or going onto the Belt were supposed to slow to fifteen miles per hour. However, this engineer had the go-go fever, for he went onto the main and was running about twenty-five or thirty mph. I got on about twelve cars back of the engine and waved good-bye to old meat-a-fest and his friends and was on the way. This train was made up of all refrigerator cars, so I had to ride the top. I got up on the catwalk on top of the car and settled down for a fast ride. This was a redball freight so the passenger and freight trains both went in the hole (went on the siding) for us all the way down the line.

The engine pulling this train was an M-1 in perfect condition so it made better than passenger train time and got nothing but green lights all the way. A green light means GO!

I talked to the fireman when we stopped in Terre Haute and he told me we had made it from a dead stop in Indianapolis to a dead stop in Terre Haute in fifty-nine minutes, a distance of seventy-two miles, and it took about five or six minutes to come around that Belt Line and get on the main line.

Yes, those old babies did indeed go down the line in those days.

CLOTHES MAKE THE MAN

There is always a way to do anything easy if you know how, but sometimes it takes a long time to learn just how to do it. I put in years looking like a typical hobo and getting run out of places and questioned by railroad dicks and harness bulls in cities and towns all over the country. One day I was in the D.&R.G.W. yards in North Cheyenne, Wyoming, watching the railroad workers going back and forth through the yards and they always spoke to each other and a few of the nicer ones even spoke to me.

An idea came to me. These guys don't all know each other personally, they are actually speaking to that standard railroad uniform. They also know I'm a hobo by the way I am dressed. I decided then and there to dress like a regular railroader and get the heat off of me for a change.

I went into the locker and shower room and saw a few guys in there bathing and changing clothes so I introduced myself and asked them if they had an old overall jacket, a pair of bib overalls, and a gray and white striped cap that they didn't need. One man said, "Yes, buddy, I think we can fix you up with some clothes and a cap." They all got busy and found two pairs of overalls, two overall jackets, a cap and about four or five old blue work shirts.

They let me take a shower and change clothes and shave. I threw my old clothes in a trash barrel and walked out of there looking like a full-blooded railroader, and I actually felt like one. I continued this camouflage as much as possible from then on and cut my bull trouble to almost zero. I even talked to a known bad dick in the yards in East Omaha, and he treated me like a brother while at the same time he was looking around for a hobo to arrest for trespassing on railroad property. I thought to myself, Good old clothes, a little deception is a wonderful thing.

I remember how good it felt to go into a store and buy a new jacket, bib overalls and a new striped cap, which I used to do now and then when I had the money to spare.

This seems to bear out the validity of the old saying "Clothes make the man."

In this case an overall jacket, a pair of bib overalls and a striped cap changed a common hobo into a respectable railroad man.

HOBO LIFE

When springtime comes with balmy days,
And green things start to growing,
I'll get my pack and bedroll ready,
For soon I must be going.

I've spent the winter in a little shack
With a hobo pal of mine,
Saw the snow piled high, heard the cold wind blow
Through the limbs of a nearby pine.

Often at night when I'm tucked in bed
I'm awakened by an approaching train,
See the golden beam of her piercing light,
Hear the whistle's sweet refrain.

Spring brings joy to a hobo's heart,
No nicer time could be,
To ride the rails on the cinder trails,
My campfire pal and me.

THE SECOND OGDEN FIASCO

I never had anything but trouble at Odgen, Utah, so I have wondered a thousand times why I ever went there in the first place. There is no answer for some things, and this is one of them, but even so, I must tell you about the second Odgen fiasco.

Both the first and second Odgen fiascoes are indeed total failures in the context that I learned the hard way that the decent people will not let you be nice and friendly and they apparently don't want you to be honest, and that's what this story is all about.

I was coming across the Great Salt Lake on that thirty-mile bridge on the U.P. main line, and a couple of other guys and I were sitting in the door of a boxcar looking at that mysterious body of salt water and wondering how it ever came to be. The salt is so dense and heavy, nothing will sink very far below the surface of the water, and this is what got me into trouble. As we were looking into the lake we saw a man in a sitting position with the top of his head about two inches below the surface of the water. He had black hair and brown eyes and was dressed in a dark suit, with a cream-colored shirt and a black tie and was wearing what appeared to be new black oxfords. Having been raised on a small farm in Indiana, I had been taught that it was every citizen's duty to report a bad accident or a killing to the law, in case it was something they didn't know about.

I said, "We must make a report about this dead man as soon as we get to Ogden."

One of my companions said, "If anyone makes a report it will be you. The less you see and the less you tell the law, the better off you are."

I considered this as a mighty poor attitude but it wasn't long until I found out how right the man was.

As soon as we got into Ogden I rushed up to the police headquarters as fast as I could, and like the little corn-fed hero that I was at that time, I told the chief of police what I had seen, and immediately he said, "Oh! So you are one of those wise guys that murders someone, then comes in and reports it, to remove the suspicion from you, heh?"

I saw the handwriting on the wall. This dummy didn't really care who did it, all he wanted was an arrest and a conviction. Some fall guy to make it look like he was really doing his job.

Silently I wished that I was ten thousand miles from there or that I had kept my mouth shut. I promised the Lord that if I came through this without getting hanged, I would never see anything again, and I have kept that promise to the Lord.

The chief had told me to sit down on a wooden chair by the wall, it was what is called a straight chair like they use for dining room chairs, and he kept me sitting there for eleven hours while he called the chief of police in every town I had ever lived in to see if I was a known criminal or was wanted in any of these towns.

This guy was the next thing to an idiot. Surely he wasn't stupid enough to believe that a wanted man or a known criminal would come to a police station to report anything, much less a murder. He got a negative answer to each long distance phone call, thank God for that.

He had sent two deputy sheriffs out to get the body and they finally returned. The coroner conducted a preliminary autopsy and found that the man had been shot through the heart at close range with a .38-caliber gun and appeared to have been dead at least fourteen hours. At the estimated time of the man's death I was in Reno or Sparks, Nevada, or perhaps somewhere in the High Sierras, coming over the hump on the way from Sacramento to Reno.

These gestapo tactics are no doubt the reason that many people refuse to cooperate with the law enforcement officers in any way.

The last thing this hard-nosed chief said was, "I guess you ain't wanted anywhere, so get the hell out of here and don't let me see you around here again."

That's the thanks I got for trying to be a good citizen.

THE MAN WITH THE WHITE EYES

I was heading west one time on the U.P. (Union Pacific) when the freight I was on pulled into Laramie, Wyoming. I decided to get off and go uptown and get something to eat. It was about 7:30 A.M. and I had been riding all night so I was hungry. As I walked along the track toward town I met a man who was sitting beside a little campfire, frying bacon and eggs and he had a one-quart coffee pot sitting in the edge of the fire boiling. As I started to pass him I spoke to him. He said, "Good morning, how are you?"

I said, "Fine, thank you, and how are you?"

He said, "I'm OK. I'm just fixing a little breakfast. Would you like to join me?"

I explained to him that I was heading for town to get something to eat, but I would rather eat with him and accepted his offer. As we ate and talked I commented that he did not look like any ordinary hobo that I had ever seen. He smiled and said, "Well, I'm not really a hobo. I'm a rancher."

I was confused for sure, so I asked, "What is a rancher doing on the road, cooking breakfast in a hobo jungle?"

He said, "I'm hunting a certain railroad detective, and when I find him I am going to blow his brains out." He hesitated for perhaps a full minute, then he said, "Three years ago this dick shot my kid brother off the top of a train, right here on this division (Cheyenne to Evanston division) and I'll never stop hunting him until I know he is dead."

I had noticed that he was wearing an overall jacket and bib overalls, a ten-gallon hat and cowboy boots, rather unusual gear for either a railroad man or a rancher, but a combination of both.

As he talked I was giving him a psychoanalysis or a character analysis perhaps, in an effort to learn more about this strange, determined, but kind-hearted man.

124

As he talked I looked him squarely in the eyes and what I saw made cold chills go up my back, for he had the lightest blue and most piercing eyes that I had ever seen. His eyes were such a light blue that they appeared to be white, and you had the feeling that they were looking completely through you. He had a sack of toppins, six big glazed donuts which we ate after we finished our bacon and egg sandwiches. When the time came for me to leave Laramie and him, I had come to feel a deep sympathy for this man and admiration for his dedication to a purpose and a principle. Few humans are like that.

As I walked away to catch that next westbound train I shook his hand and thanked him for his hospitality, and cautioned him to be careful and said that I hope we meet again sometime. I have never seen him since, but there is one thing I am sure of, I am glad that I am not the man who killed his brother.

After we had eaten and were just sitting there talking, he said, "I'll show you what that fellow is going to get a mess of." He reached under the bib of his overalls and pulled out a fully loaded .45 Colt six-shooter and held it out for my observation. Then he said, "I always wear a suit under these overalls, so that I can mix with any crowd."

He dropped the overall bib and unbuttoned the jacket and sure enough, there was a blue serge suit, a white shirt and tie. All of which made me know that this man wasn't an image maker or a glory-hunting windbag, he was putting it plain, simple and true. This would indeed be someone to reckon with if he was angry at you!

DINGBATS ON THE ROAD

You meet all kinds of dingbats wherever you are, and it has been my misfortune to meet more than my share. I'll tell you a story about one of these ding-a-lings that could have cost me my life if the Old Man up above had not been looking after me.

I came out of Des Moines, Iowa, one time on the Rock Island Railroad, and there were perhaps forty or fifty bos on that train from all over the country, and I thought we were all heading for Chicago, as it turned out one young man's folks had a farm about twenty-five or thirty miles east of Des Moines and he decided to make a quick stop and go see his mom and dad.

The train was a slow freight so it was only running about forty-five mph and this is no doubt what kept some of us from getting killed.

When this guy saw his old home place come in sight he got down on the catwalk on an oil tanker and closed the valve on the main air line. This throws the back section of the train brakes into emergency and slides every wheel from where you cut the valve off, back to the caboose, the crummy.

In turn, this also cuts the train in two, which allows the engine and x number of cars to go on while the back part of the train and caboose comes to a sudden dead stop.

I don't know whether this guy jumped off or fell off, but when I got straightened up I saw him down there beside the railroad grinning all over his face, as the saying goes.

I got down on the ground and started hollering as loud as I could. "Let's get to hell out of here before we get twenty years in the pen for what that dingbat did."

Cutting a train in two like that used to carry an automatic twenty-year sentence.

126

Three or four guys and I ran over into a woods and hid. I kept seeing cars and trucks going by about half a mile south of that woods so I knew there was some kind of a highway over there. I finally got up and told those guys that I was going over to that highway and hitchhike for the next fifty to a hundred miles, until I got out of this part of the country.

I hadn't been on the highway over five minutes when a truck picked me up and took me into Moline, Illinois. I was safe once again and I wasn't really any worse off for going through this ordeal.

OLD YELLOW HAIR, REEFER, AND FRIENDS

My old buddy Wade Palmer, Yellow Hair as we used to call him, lived a thousand years and died at the age of forty-two. Wade was never married and never even got very serious about any woman. There were women in his life, but they were just friends and in many cases just the one night stand sort of thing. Wade was a professional hobo of the first water.

He used to say, "Reefer, I've rode every railroad in the country so many times that I've got a controlling interest in most all of them."

When he was home in Terre Haute, Indiana, he lived with his sister and brother-in-law, but he wasn't home very often. His sister used to try to get him to settle down for she viewed hoboing as just a wild streak that possessed some young men and would or should soon pass. She didn't understand.

Wade died at home and because he was at home.

The water pipes froze under his sister's house and he went under there in subzero weather to thaw them out and died two days later of pneumonia.

When I was at home in Terre Haute, I stayed with the old Cherokee Indian woman who partly raised me. It was a poor home but a good home, where I was always welcome.

That old lady washed for people and did the ironing if they requested it, but I never knew her to get more than three dollars for the largest family washing and ironing, and when you washed on a washboard by hand and did the ironing with sadirons that she heated on top of the cookstove winter and summer, that was work, hard work. She is dead now but I am sure the Lord had a special place for her when she got there.

I have seen her give some hobo the last bite of food she had in the house and do it from the goodness of her heart. I asked her about it once and she said, "Son, you must always trust the Lord in all things. If you give your last food away to someone who is hungry, the Lord will also provide for you when it comes time for you to eat, and it does indeed work. I have actually seen it work many times."

I have seen her give away the last morsel of food in the morning and she didn't have any promise of getting anything for us to eat, and I'll swear by all that's holy that before dark came there would be something totally unexpected show up and we would have a sufficient amount of food in the house when bedtime came.

The above articles accurately describe the homes of Wade Palmer ("Yellow Hair") and I, Charles E. Fox ("Reefer Charlie"), homes we were grateful for in spite of the fact that we were incurable hoboes.

Long before the song "Everybody Loves Somebody" came out Yellow Hair and I learned the meaning and value of these words. When we were sitting by a little campfire in the jungle at Natchez, Mississippi, or at Wausaw, Wisconsin, it always was reassuring to know that you had a home somewhere and someone that cared about you.

WHERE DID THEY GO?

Once when I was hitchhiking in northern Wisconsin near the town of Green Valley I ran into a strange thing. As I walked along the forest-lined highway I noticed that a bad storm was coming up, so I began to look for some kind of shelter. I eventually came to a little log cabin, sitting back about two hundred feet from the side of the road.

I decided to go in and ask these folks if they would let me stay in their house until the storm was over.

I went to the back door and started to knock, then I realized that the door was standing open about eight or ten inches. I peeped inside and could tell that the house hadn't been occupied for some time, so I went in and made myself at home.

I immediately noticed a strange thing. The table had been set and three people had been eating, when something had interrupted their meal. From the condition of the food I guessed that they had been gone at least three or four months. There was dried food in each plate and the coffee cups had all been partly full when they left. The coffee had evaporated but each cup had a brown coffee stain covering the sides of the cups to the level of the coffee that had been left in the cups when these folks left so suddenly.

There was a dish half-full of rice that had dried out and shriveled up, a Pet Milk can that was half-full of dried milk, and a half a loaf of bread that was as hard as a rock.

There was a tablespoon and a dish rag lying on the floor and one chair was overturned, otherwise everything seemed to be in order.

I had an uneasy feeling. Something out of the ordinary had happened here. There was a little vegetable garden spot on the west side of the house, but aside from the small clearing the place was surrounded by dense woods.

After the storm was over I went out and looked around to see if I could find any graves or skeletons that might hold the secret to what had happened here. I searched for an hour or more but found nothing, so I left.

To this day, forty-two years later, I still think about it and wonder what really happened that morning in that little cabin near Green Valley, Wisconsin, for it is reasonable to assume that they were eating breakfast when for some unknown reason they left the table when they were only halfway through their meal.

Maybe nothing bad happened, I hope not, but it looked pretty strange to me.

Throughout this book I have taken you to many faraway places which I visited for one reason only, the desire to see America. I was raised by poor people, so traveling and visiting the scenic spots of America was out of the question. None of my family on either side of the house (the older ones) ever had a vacation of any kind, so I decided to make up for all that they had been deprived of.

THE FAST BUCK HUSTLERS

Tourists spend millions of dollars every year to see a lot less than I saw for free. The only time the fast buck hustlers didn't try to hustle me was when I was on the bum, a hobo.

I don't have any use for a conniver of any kind, for they are worse than an honest thief. I knew one guy who used to meet the troop trains in the depots and take up a collection from returning wounded veterans or guys that were on their way overseas with the promise to go get them some whiskey, and as soon as he collected twenty-five or thirty dollars he would disappear and they were out of x number of dollars and didn't get any whiskey either.

Hoboes stole a "gump" (chicken) or a watermelon now and then, but I never heard of a real hobo taking advantage of someone less fortunate than himself. This "collector" told me he was sorry when World War Two ended, for it cut off his source of easy money. Yes, friend, there are a lot of people that are worse than any hobo that ever lived.

THE SWITCH DOLLY DIVE

I went into the Big 4 yards at East St. Louis, Illinois one night and the word was out on the road that the Brooklyn Yard at East St. Louis was "ranked," meaning that there were some unfriendly dicks or bulls that would bear watching.

Little Chuck Lehman and I were together and had talked the situation over long before we got there, so when the train went into the east end of the yards and started to slow down a little we decided to unload.

Chuck got off first and as soon as I saw that he was OK I got off. The train was still running pretty fast to get off at night, thirty or forty mph perhaps. They had just rebuilt the road bed with crushed limestone and that was my undoing.

When I hit the ground I was running as fast as I could in an effort to stay upright. The farther I ran the more I leaned over forward, until I became overbalanced and fell flat on my stomach. I slid about ten feet and hit an iron switch dolly hard enough to kill a Missouri mule. Fortunately I hit one of the arms of the cross with my left shoulder and that stopped me instantly. A switch dolly is one of those iron cross affairs that they have at every switch and is an indicator to show whether the switch is open or closed.

The arms of the dolly are flat steel stampings about eighteen inches long, five inches wide, and three-sixteenths inches thick and are shaped somewhat like an arrowhead. They are pointed at one end and have a V notch cut into the other end. If I had hit that pointed end it would have gone completely through me and the notched end would have done about as much damage. Luckily I hit the flat side of an arm with my shoulder, so other than getting a badly bruised shoulder I didn't get hurt.

133

When Little Chuck saw what had happened it nearly scared him out of his wits, but when I jumped up and said, "I'm OK!" he gave a big sigh of relief. When we got to town we went into a public toilet and he looked at my shoulder and shook his head. He said, "You know, kid, the good Lord is looking after you."

A PISTOL-PACKING MAMA

B ack in the early 1930s fashionable young ladies began wearing man-style white shirts and white
slacks for casual street wear. I saw two gals dressed
like this one afternoon in Butte, Montana. Two gals that I
soon wished I had never met.

There was a freight train all made up and about ready to
head east, so I climbed into a boxcar where I could stretch
out and have a more pleasant ride and get a few hours of
restful sleep. I had just got up in the car and straightened
up when I saw these two gals dressed in white sitting on a
piece of cardboard and leaning back against the wall of
the car.

I spoke to them and they spoke. Then the big one, a redhead, reached down into the front of her shirt and pulled
out a small revolver, a .32 I think.

She said, "Now mister, let me give you a piece of good ad-
vice. You get down in the other end of the car and stay there
until you get ready to get off. If you even try to bother either
of us I will kill you."

I said, "Just hold it a minute, I'm not in the habit of mo-
lesting women nor men, so you have nothing to fear."

She said, "I don't fear you at all, I'm just warning you
about what will happen to you if you try anything."

They got off somewhere, about seventy-five or a hundred
miles east of Butte, and that's the last I ever saw of them. I
can assure you that I rested a lot better after that pistol-
packing redhead and her buddy were gone.

THE MEDICINE
OF STATE HOUSE PARK

When I was down in Georgia, Florida, and Alabama one time I contracted a bad case of asthma in one of those states, but I have never been able to figure out which state gave it to me. I have a hunch that it might have been Georgia, but I'm not sure. As the months passed I got progressively worse, until I reached the point where I had to sleep sitting up. I decided to go to Arizona, as I had known of cases where asthmatic people had gone down there and gotten completely well within a short time.

I hitchhiked down there in order to stay as clean as I could, and you sure can't stay clean when you are riding trains.

I got into Phoenix about noon on a Monday and being in possession of a little money and not having sense enough to be trusted with such a commodity I immediately pulled a boo-boo. Instead of checking the town out to try to establish a sensible economic course to take, I went down on Campbell Avenue and rented a furnished room and paid two weeks' rent in advance eight dollars. I went for a walk and wound up in the state house grounds, sort of a beautiful parklike affair covered with huge palm trees. U.S. Route 80 ran along in front of the state house at that time so this State House Park was quite a popular spot in those days. I sat down under a palm tree and started talking to a man from Nebraska who was there for the same reason I was. He had suffered with asthma for years. I asked him if the hot dry climate seemed to be helping him?

He said, "Lord yes, I'm 100 percent better and I've only been here three weeks. I can't remember when I could breathe like this," and he took a deep breath to illustrate what he meant.

He had done the same thing I did. He had rented a room somewhere but had slept in that park every night since he had been in Phoenix, and I also wound up doing the same thing.

Our room rent was a total loss.

The second night I went up to the park to go to bed, I ran into a couple of young women from New Orleans, Louisiana, and they were also living in the park and had been for four or five weeks. They didn't have asthma, but they had discovered that the park was a good place for any wandering gee-bobo to live, especially on hot nights in Arizona.

Being attracted to the opposite sex to some extent, I soon became most friendly with these two queens. I started meeting them up there in the park every evening and we would spend the night pretty close to each other. We did not sleep together, but we all slept under the same palm tree. After a few nights it occurred to me that I had never seen this biggest gal without a silk scarf on her head.

Being a tactful man I asked her point-blank. "What do you do, wear that head scarf all the time?"

She said, "Yes, and I have worn one for the last two years."

I looked at her and debated whether I should ask her why? She must have read my mind, for she said, "I'll tell you why I wear it, I am completely bald."

She was a nice-looking gal and I found it hard to believe that she could be totally bald and hide it so cleverly with just a scarf.

I asked, "Are you totally bald?"

She said, "Yes, I am."

Then she reached up and pulled the scarf off and I saw that she didn't have a hair on her head.

I asked her what happened and she said that she had typhoid fever two years ago and all her hair fell out. She said she had lain at death's door for five weeks in a New Orleans hospital. She put the scarf back on and asked, "Now that you know, do you still like me?"

That got me, so I said, "Heavens yes, what has that got to do with whether I like you or dislike you?"

These girls said they were eventually going to wind up in Hollywood where they planned to go to work as domestics.

The climate was helping my problem and it did not take long to do it, for on the twelfth morning it was as though I had never had asthma, I was a new man. I bid my erstwhile friends good-bye and headed west on Route 80 toward Yuma and the Imperial Valley where you could usually pick up a few days' work on a ranch or farm, but keep in mind that the folks out there don't like that word "farm." Everything is a "ranch" even if it is only a quarter-acre tract and all they are raising is marigolds.

I never saw those two girls again, but I hope they did OK wherever they went. I am also grateful that to date I haven't had to sleep sitting up since I made that trip to sunny Phoenix.

138

THE ROCKS OF BLACK RIVER

Once when I was traveling with a family from the East who were going to California, we stopped at a little campground on the Black River near Melbourne, Arkansas, to rest up and get some dinner. I walked out to the center of the river bridge and was looking down at the water and thinking how I would like to go swimming and get cooled off.

While I was standing there an old man came up the river in an old johnboat and I could see that he was a riverman, probably a trotline and D-net fisherman who had made his living along this river for fifty or sixty years.

Most rivermen won't lie to you about the river, but this old gent put it on me but good.

I spoke to him and then asked him about the water around that middle bridge pier, how deep it was and if there was anything in there to bump my head on if I dove off that pier?

He said, "That water is a good twelve feet deep and there's nothing in there to get hurt on, so you can dive and swim all you want to. Wish I was younger, I'd go in with you."

I thanked him and we said good-bye, and he went on back down the river, to his camp I suppose.

I went back to the car and got my bathing trunks out of my pack, went up the riverbank behind a big tree and put them on. I went back out to the center of the bridge and climbed down onto the pier.

The top of the pier was about four or five feet above the water, which is just a nice dive, ordinarily!

I dove and hit a flat rock as big as a dining room table which was about three feet below the surface of the water. I hit that rock so hard that my arms folded up and the top of my head hit squarely on the flat top of that rock and I thank the Lord that rock was flat and smooth, for any size or kind of projection would have torn the top of my head wide open.

The folks I was with were watching and said, "Your legs were sticking straight up out of the water and quivering, and you stood on your head fifteen or twenty seconds then you put your feet down and stood up on the rock."

My neck was almost broken. I finally laid down in the water and swam to the bank and sat there for a while until I recovered. If I could have gotten my hands on that old man right then, I would have beat him into a pulp.

I was sore and stiff for several weeks, and even to this day I cannot turn my head to either side to any degree, so I have a hard time seeing where I'm going when I am backing a car. I guess I'm lucky that I can even see straight ahead, for by all rights I should have died right there in Arkansas's beautiful Black River.

THE EFFINGHAM FLYING BATH

Little Chuck Lehman and I caught the first blind on a passenger train at Terre Haute one night and started for St. Louis. They were double heading two K-4s on this baby so we knew she was going to move on when she got out of town, and that's what we wanted.

Those Pennsy passenger trains and some freights took water on the fly in those days. All went well until we got to Effingham, Illinois, then it happened, I got a bath. There was a water trough in the middle of the track at Effingham, so this train slowed down to about forty-five mph to take water. The fireman dropped that water scoop down when we got over the trough and about ten seconds later about seventy-five gallons of water came back in that blind and nearly drowned me.

Little Chuck caught some of it, but naturally I caught the most, as usual.

In those days I always seemed to be in the wrong place at the wrong time. I could have killed that little louse, for he laughed all the way to East St. Louis about me getting soaked.

You can believe me when I say that I was very careful from then on. I stayed away from all trains that took water on the fly.

UNWRITTEN LAW OF THE WEST

In the West there has always been an unwritten law ever since cattle ranching became a business. All cowboys and ranch hands will have two things, even if they don't have anything else. These two things are the best hat and boots he can afford to buy. I have seen many instances where a man would pay two or three months' wages for a fine Stetson hat or a fancy pair of hand-tooled boots.

In those days the average cowhand got from twenty to thirty dollars a month and his board and room, so these hats and boots were pretty expensive.

I came out of Cheyenne one time on the D.&R.G.W. heading for Denver. This freight was made up of nothing but ore cars that were going to the ore mines in southern Colorado, so I climbed up into one of the low-sided cars and resigned myself to a stand-up ride all the way to Denver. Other men got on, even two guys with their wives, and we headed south. I noticed that we had a tall cowboy with a beautiful white Stetson and a highly polished pair of fancy boots on, new dungarees (blue jeans nowadays), a light suede jacket and a hand-stitched western shirt.

He and I got to talking and he told me that he had saved up sixty dollars and was heading for Denver to spend a week just doing nothing but enjoying himself.

The train kept picking up speed with each passing mile, so by the time we were ten or twelve miles south of Cheyenne those ore cars were bouncing around like a cork on the ocean. The steam engine pulling that train was old and it wasn't very large as engines go, but that "Old Hog" would really run. We were rolling sixty-five or seventy all the way.

As we were going around the foot of a low mountain in an area that was totally barren of vegetation of any kind, I heard the cowboy exclaim, "Damn the luck!"

I turned to see what had happened and I saw his new Stetson flying through the air about fifty feet west of the train, then it fell to the ground and started rolling over and over like a tumbleweed.

The hat was gone, for the man never lived that could get off that train without getting killed.

He said, "Well, there's two months' wages shot to hell."

I sympathized with him, but there was nothing I could do. But I know one thing, someone wound up with a good hat for free.

I SAW THEM
IN THE MOONLIGHT

L ittle Chuck Lehman and I came out of Terre Haute one
afternoon on the Big 4 Railroad, on a slow freight
that was picking up and setting off cars at every
town of any size. It stopped in Paris, Illinois, and set off a
few cars and picked up a few, but so far they hadn't bothered the empty boxcar we were riding in.

We pulled out of Paris at dusk and as we were pulling
back on the main line two big Negroes jumped up into the
car. We all spoke to each other and they went down to the
other end of the car and sat down.

Chuck and I had found us a couple pieces of heavy wrapping paper to roll up in when we went to bed. Just before we
retired he whispered to me and said, "We better sleep light,
those guys might be up to something."

We rolled up in our paper and were soon asleep. Some
time later something awakened me, so I didn't move. I just
opened my eyes and there in that patch of moonlight were
those two black men on hands and knees, slipping up on us.

I pressed my elbow against Chuck's back and he reached
back quietly and pressed on my elbow. I knew he was
awake, so I got my pocketknife out and opened it quietly
and waited. Thinking we were asleep our visitors came a
little closer. Chuck started snoring gently and they came
on. When they got just right Little Chuck sat up suddenly
and hit the nearest one squarely in the mouth with the
barrel of that .32-20 automatic that he carried. The man
howled in pain and they both leaped to their feet and so did
we. Chuck fired one shot between their heads, then told
them to go to the door of the car. They complied and he told
them to jump out on the ground. They hesitated a few sec-

onds and Chuck took a quick step and hit the biggest one in the side of the head and knocked him ten feet out into a field, then he turned to the other one and asked, "Do you want some of that or would you rather I shot you?"

The man said, "No man, I'll jump!" And jump he did.

Chuck turned to me and said, "I knew they were going to try to take us when they came in the door. There's good and bad in all races and the best thing to do is handle the bad ones rough."

Then he added, "You know, kid, I would have killed them both if they had given me any trouble."

And he would have, for I knew this little five-foot Dutchman.

Two or three months later we saw these two men down on Market Street (skid row) in St. Louis and they acted as though they had never seen us before, and that was fine with us.

THE KINGDOM OF MARKET
AND BROADWAY

One time when I was in St. Louis on skid row I was walking down Market Street smoking a cigarette. At the corner of Sixth and Market I stopped, took another inhale and threw the cigarette butt down on the sidewalk. A man that was standing there picked the butt up and put it in his mouth, took a full pack of Lucky Strikes out of his pocket and laid them on top of the corner mailbox and walked on down the street smoking that butt. I picked the pack of Luckies up and put them in my pocket and walked on down the street.

I told Chuck about it and showed him the Luckies. He said, "Kid, a damned junkie will do anything. That guy was probably a snow bird [meaning a cocaine addict]."

At that time Market and Broadway was the very center of "all that was" in America, for sooner or later all the hoboes, all the boosters, all the thieves, and all the junkies showed up there.

This used to be a meeting place and it was not uncommon for two bos in Frisco to agree in August to meet at Market and Broadway the fifteenth of next May or the next Fourth of July.

We all knew that this section of St. Louis was run by the Egan Mob and the Green Boys.

If a tramp knew Bill Green, Chippie Robinson or Dinty Colbeck, he didn't have a thing in the world to worry about. They were good people.

The Harness Bulls never bothered anyone around Market and Broadway as long as they didn't get drunk and start using tools (guns and knives).

There was a real good jungle out at ninety hundred North

Broadway, alongside the Wabash Railroad yards, next to the river (Mississippi).

The place to avoid in those days was ninety hundred South Broadway. That was the St. Louis County workhouse, and it was about as bad as Arkansas's Tucker Farm.

I went down by there one day and the guys that worked in the stone quarry had caught a big possum. They gave it to me and I took it over on Fourth Street and got a colored lady to bake it with potatoes and gravy and we put on a feed. It was a treat to watch those kids of hers go after that possum, gravy, and potatoes.

I guess from what they said that was the first good meal they had sat down to in a long time.

THE HOBO ARISTOCRAT

You don't see many people like some of the old-time hoboes that I used to know. Most of these guys were strictly one of a kind. Some of them were comedian-type characters that would make Bob Hope get up and dig deep to keep up with them. There were others who were the strong silent type guys who always did the listening while you did the talking. There were hotheads, mean characters that some good guy would wind up having to bounce a club off their heads sooner or later.

Many of those mean ones were found lying along the side of some railroad dead. But by and large the average hobo was a pretty decent sort of person.

One guy I used to laugh at every time I saw him was old "If you can hit it, you can eat it" Johnny Woods. He was something else. At one time he had a home and a mother and father and all the family ties that any ordinary person has, but by the time I met him he had even forgotten where he was born and who his parents were. No, that is just a wisecrack, but it is true that to my knowledge he never mentioned anything about his family nor his childhood.

Another thing that made him unusual was the fact that he spent the greater part of his life within an area about two hundred miles square, with St. Louis as the hub of the area, yet as a hobo and as a tramp it would be safe to say that he must have traveled at least half a million miles and he wasn't on the road over 50 percent of his time.

He used to hang around Alton and Woodriver quite a lot and it was in these towns that he used to throw his periodical protracted drunks.

Ray Milan became famous with the "lost weekend," Johnny Woods should have been a hundred times as famous, for he usually lost five or six months out of each year.

They say that opposites attract each other so this accounts for the fact Johnny's lifelong road buddy was Irish Bobby McCoy, the aristocrat of hoboes, a man who never took a drink of booze in his life. Bobby used to stay dressed up most of the time. He usually wore a suit, dress oxfords and spats and always a stiff kady hat and a dress shirt and tie.

Dressing this way was Bobby's trademark, getting these fancy duds was simpler than one would imagine. Bobby visited used clothing stores, the Salvation Army, the Goodwill Stores, and even pawn shops. These were all good sources of clothes for an aristocrat.

I met Bobby one time on Collinsville Avenue in east St. Louis and he was wearing a frock tailcoat and was even carrying a silver mounted cane. I had to laugh. He said he bought the cane for a buck at a house sale.

When Johnny got sober and he and Bobby decided to go on the road for a while, they always took a young man by the name of Jimmie Burns with them to bird dog for them (do the chores, run errands and serve as a lookout in their jungle camps). This Jimmie Burns was one of the finest human beings that ever lived. He was soft-spoken and gentle, polite and friendly, but he was one of the few men I have ever met that was totally without fear of anything in the world.

HEIR TO EADS BRIDGE

James Eads Howe who went by the road name of J. B. King, whose mother had been an Eads and had married a man named Howe, was a common hobo like the rest of us, to all outward appearances, but he was unique in the context that he was the grandchild of James Eads, and as such was sole heir to the Eads Bridge at St. Louis, Missouri, and to his grandfather's fortune. He used his road name J. B. King to save his family from embarrassment.

He was sitting in the jungle at Granite City, Illinois, making a pot of coffee in a half-gallon molasses bucket when a lawyer appeared on the scene and informed him that his grandfather had passed away and that he had been named as sole heir to the toll bridge and half a million dollars in cash.

J. B. accepted it like a gentleman and left to consummate the terms of the will and to appoint a competent lawyer to manage his business interests, then he returned to the jungle and died years later as a millionaire hobo.

ABALONE BAY

Dedicated to Euell Gibbons

I wouldn't be caught dead in old Merced,
And the same goes for L.A.
But I can spend my life and enjoy myself,
On the shores of Abalone Bay.

A driftwood fire and a pocketknife,
To open those protective shells.
And cook that meat so I can eat,
By the blue Pacific swells.

TERRE HAUTE BOS, TRAMPS, AND BOOSTERS

There were a lot of hoboes around Terre Haute years ago, and believe me some of them were characters, but most of them were pretty good guys so long as you treated them right.

There was old Mungo Penman (the barber) and old Buttons, who got his name from selling ten cent cards of buttons to make his living. Then there was "Horse Radish" Charlie Wilson, who tried to make enough horse radish in spring to carry him through the rest of the year.

Many tramps used to pick up junk in gunnysacks and this is the way many made their living.

One of the Terre Haute bums as the decent people called us, that I used to buddy around with a lot was Wayne Brennan, more commonly known as "Diddildy Dido George." Wayne was a jungle booster, a jug bum, or a member of the Funnel Gang and the Bingaloo Gang of old Terre Haute's infamous west side or Tenderloin District, which President Hoover slowly but surely turned into skid row. Even the prostitutes were on the bum half of the time, and the precinct committeemen worked two days a week for the county trustee, for a two-dollar-and-fifty-cent grocery order.

There was a vacant lot at Second and Cherry streets in Terre Haute years ago where a man by the name of Colonel Crawford winter quartered his road show.

He had a small zoo there the year around, as well as all of his circus and carnival equipment. He sold herb medicines, rattlesnake oil, and a dozen other things on his road tours every summer. A friend found him dead in 1930.

It wasn't long until everything he had was gone. The humane society did something with his animals and someone else did something with his wagons and so on, until nothing was left. By 1931 the lot was totally vacant and soon grew up in weeds.

It wasn't long until the tramps, hoboes, winos, and jake leg boys took it over. There were also a goodly population of cut alchy specialists hanging out there.

We were all over there one afternoon heisting a jug (drinking bootleg alcohol) when some well-dressed man came in and asked, "Is Bob Logan around?"

We didn't know who he was so no one answered his question. This could be a plainclothesman, or a fink bent on putting old Bob in jail for something. Only those who have been all the way down the road know how these alleged "decent people" will frame a drunk or a tramp on some trumped-up charge just to get him off the street for a while. This statement does not apply to all policemen nor to all common citizens, but it does apply to about 10 percent of the general public.

The man stood and looked at us, then it dawned on him what he had did wrong. To get information you must introduce yourself honestly.

He said, "I am an attorney, Mr. So and So and I am Bob's dad's attorney. I must find him, for he has came into a sizable inheritance."

Frisco Jack leaned over and shook a guy that was lying on the ground asleep and drunk not two feet from where the attorney was standing. Frisco shook the man and said, "Hey Bob, get up, there's an attorney here to see you."

Bob finally sat up and looked at the attorney, wondering why a lawyer would want to see him.

He finally got up and combed his hair and asked the lawyer what he had on his mind.

The lawyer said, "Let's go down to my office and I'll explain all the details to you, and there are some papers you will have to sign."

Bob eventually came back at dusk and he was cold sober.

He said, "Boys, old Bob is going to start living and change

his whole life-style. I just inherited a million and a quarter dollars!"

We all sat there with our mouths open, staring in disbelief at our old buddy.

Was this Bob Logan the tramp, the jug booster, the eternal good guy, who had slept in old sheds, empty houses, weed patches, under bridges, and even in jails with us nights without number? There was a long pause, for effect no doubt, for Bob was first, last and always a showman.

Finally he said, "You won't believe it, but I just found out that I was or am Old John 'Hominy' Godsey's son and sole heir. My mother came to work for John Godsey when she was a young girl, as a prostitute, and John fell in love with her. The love affair went on for years and she had a baby by him, and the baby was me. All through these years he was living with his wife, Lillian [Diamond Tooth Lil], so nothing was ever mentioned about him being my father. My mother knew and he knew. My mother died when I was ten years old and I was placed in an orphan's home. Old Hominy used to come to see me once in awhile and he always brought me some candy and gave me a few bucks. I thought it was just because he knew my mother for so long and knew me since the day I was born. He never told me a thing about his real reason for coming to see me. Diamond Tooth Lil finally died and Old John continued to operate his sporting houses, but his last years were lonely and miserable. I stayed at the orphan's home until I was fifteen years old, then I ran away and became a tramp. Later on I became a drunk by choice, for I didn't have much to live for, as you all know."

Then he said, "I've got to go to court tomorrow and change my name to Robert Logan Godsey, and from then on I'll be Bob Godsey."

We didn't see him for three or four days and when he did show up at Colonel Crawford's lot he was dressed up like the duke of Macaroni. He had a haircut and a shave, and a bath, a seventy-five-dollar suit, Stetson hat, Florsheim oxfords, white shirt and black tie. What a difference a little soap and water, a barber, and a few clothes can make.

He told us as he was getting ready to leave, "I'm going to set you guys up to a grand wingding before I leave. I want you to have a good time and I want you all to behave yourselves and stay together."

He told us he was taking off for Coral Gables, Florida in a few days, "So if I don't see you anymore all of you be careful and remember that I am always your friend and I'll miss all of you, but it's better for me that I change my way of living and my address at the same time. So long!"

He was gone. A short time later a delivery man came with a case of pints of Seagrams "7" whiskey and as he was leaving a pickup truck came with six cases of cold Champagne Velvet beer and enough longhorn cheese, cold cuts of meat and round buns to feed an army. What a blowout. We never saw him again, but thanks to Robert Logan Godsey.

THE SOUP WAS TOO RICH FOR ME

As the old saying goes, quote: "Some days it don't even pay you to get up." I have had quite a few of those days, one of which I will endeavor to tell you about, and you can take it for whatever it is worth.

One time when my brother Frank and I were on the bum and in the poorest country or I should say city on earth, we were going through some pretty lean days. We were sitting under a railroad bridge talking and both of us were about starved, so we decided to go into town to a place called the Lighthouse Mission and see if we could ding them out of a hot meal.

We got there just when they were serving supper, and they had vegetable soup. It looked and smelled wonderful, so we really perked up.

We got our free lunch ticket and went through the line and they gave us a big bowl of soup and two slices of second-day bread. We found a place to sit at a big long board table. We salt and peppered the soup to taste, then broke the bread up into small pieces and put it in the soup.

They had given us small tablespoons to eat with, so we tore into that soup like two wild men going through a buckberry patch. I finished eating first and was sitting there at peace with the world. I was even thinking this wasn't such a bad world after all. All of a sudden my stomach turned a flip and I jumped up and ran out into the alley. I was so sick I had to lean against the side of the building to keep from falling. I heaved up everything but my internal organs. I looked at this mess to try to determine what had made me sick, and there in the middle of that soup was the biggest black fly that I have ever seen. He had fallen into the pot when it was cooking, so he was thoroughly cooked, but he was too rich for my blood.

We left and neither of us ever ate in a mission nor any type of a ding shop again.

A trip or two like this will make a vegetarian and a raw food eater out of anyone.

THAT IMPORTANT
BRAKE SHOE KEY

Back in 1929 when I first went on the road and was almost totally green about anything connected with life on the road, I had an experience that I never forgot. Little Chuck Lehman and I were crossing Illinois on the Big 4 Railroad. When we got into the boxcar that we were going to ride, Chuck looked at the door of the car and pulled on it. He said, "It's OK, I won't have to sprag it." I did not know what he was talking about, for I figured if he said it was all right it must be.

We took off down the main and everything was going just fine. The train was running about fifty or fifty-five miles an hour so we were getting across the country.

Chuck and I were sitting on the floor and leaning back against the wall smoking and talking, when all of a sudden the engineer slammed on the brakes and the door slammed shut and locked.

Chuck muttered something about "Damn the luck, I should have put a key in there."

I didn't know what he was talking about. All I could think of was, how are we going to get out of here?

The train finally stopped in some town and we stood by the door and listened. Finally we heard someone walking along past the car. We kicked on the door and hollered. A brakeman opened the door and said, "So she went shut and locked on you, eh?"

We said, "Yes," and thanked him for opening the door. We got out on the ground and Chuck said, "I'll show you something, kid. That was a rube stunt letting that door go shut."

He hunted around on the ground and came up with an old brake shoe key, then he pushed the door back as far as it would go and wedged the brake shoe key into the track that the door ran on. He said, "That's the first thing you always want to do when you are going to ride in an empty boxcar, wedge the door open." In the years that followed, I never forgot this lesson. To learn by making mistakes is a sure way to learn, but it is a hard way.

THE AMAZING MEN
OF THE ROAD

During my early years on the road I never ceased to be amazed at the men I met on the road. It seemed to me that about seven out of every ten men were unusually brilliant in one way or another and all were worldly wise and experienced travelers. Some of the greatest philosophers and artists I ever met were hoboes or tramps. Many were of the Eric Hoffer type of rough outspoken but strictly honest men. When you think of it honestly and in its proper perspective, what mode of life could be more conducive to philosophy than a life spent on the road?

I have seen some of these men take a lead pencil and two or three pieces of crayons of different colors and create a beautiful picture of some kind on the wall of a boxcar or on a common paper sack. I have met many fine musicians on the road. One old man was a piano player that was definitely a genius. He could play anything from folk and country music to popular and classic masterpieces and do it all without any sheet music to go by. This was how he made his living. He would play for anyone who had a piano in their home if they would give him a meal. I went by a place one time and heard someone playing religious songs and the music was beautiful. I sat down in a little park across the street to listen. The music finally stopped and a few minutes later the old man came walking out with a lump (a big package of food) wrapped in a newspaper. He was thanking the people for the food and they actually invited him to come back any time.

THE HOBO PREACHER

I met another old man three or four times who was a preacher deluxe. I firmly believe that he knew the entire Protestant Bible by heart. He carried a small bundle, like nearly all real hoboes and tramps, but his trademark was the well-used medium-sized Bible that he carried in his hand or under his arm incessantly. This was one of those unusual deals that happens now and then, and here is why it was unusual.

When I was eleven years old we lived beside the Cloverleaf Railroad, about two miles west of Kokomo, Indiana. One evening an old man came along, he was walking along the railroad track, which was graded up to a height of perhaps fifteen feet. My dad was out in the yard so the old man hollered down and asked him if there was a chance of getting something to eat.

My dad said, "Yes, sir, come on down. My wife is fixing supper now."

The old man came down and my dad took him in the house so he could wash up and comb his hair and be ready to eat. After the old man had finished cleaning up he said, "I am a minister of the Gospel, so if you folks believe in God and don't mind, I would like to read a few passages from the Bible and have a moment of prayer before we eat."

My dad said, "You just hop to it, I think it might do us all good."

This was in 1924 and this man was at least seventy years old at that time, but he was physically active and mentally young and alert, and what a preacher he was!

There were no hell fire and brimstone scare stories, so we all enjoyed the short program. We ate and our guest sat around and talked to us for perhaps an hour, then he asked us to say a short prayer with him before he left. We went out into the yard and watched him climb up the side of that steep railroad embankment. When he got to the top he turned and smiled and waved his hand at us and walked north up the railroad and was soon out of sight.

This was five years before I went on the road, and at that time being a hobo was the farthest thing from my mind.

How little we know of what life has in store for us! I was destined to meet this old man two or three times in the next few years, and each time I saw him he had his little bindle in one hand and his Bible in the other. I saw him off and on until about 1936 or '37, then I never saw him again, so I presume he had died.

THE HOBO HORSE DOCTOR

Before I had been on the road very long I learned that a good many hoboes and tramps had a good working knowledge of the art of healing. I have seen these hobo medicine men practically perform miracles with some of the simplest treatments of medication imaginable.

My first experience with hobo medicine was when I was about eight or nine years old. My dad had a horse that had been kicked on the left shoulder, which caused the shoulder to swell badly and caused the horse to become lame. My dad sharpened the little blade of his knife to a razor edge and lanced the swelling directly in the center. He made about a one-inch incision. When he pressed on the swelling a quantity of blood and puss came out, then out came a clot of blood the size of a large orange.

He had been opening that incision and letting the shoulder drain and injecting medicine with a horse syringe every day for two weeks, but the injury didn't seem to be healing.

We were out there working on the shoulder one afternoon when a tramp came along and stopped to watch us. He started inquiring about the injury and noted that it should have been healed by now.

My dad and him got to talking about it and the tramp said, "If I tell you how to heal that wound easy and quick, will you give me some supper?"

My dad said, "Hell yes, I'll even let you stay here for three or four days and help me treat the wound!"

The tramp was, as I know now, a man in his early thirties, but at that time I thought he was an old man. He said, "Have your wife brown some flour in a dry skillet, and we will fill that incision full of flour while it is warm. Then we will get some water and make a paste of some of the flour and cover the entire swollen area."

163

If I had not seen it, I would not believe it, but I assure you that what I am going to tell you is true. Within three days all the swelling was gone, the drainage had stopped and the healing process was well advanced.

My dad was so impressed that he asked this traveling horse doctor to stick around for two or three weeks.

One morning the tramp said, "Well, Foxie, I'll be going today and I want to thank you for being so nice to me!"

My dad said, "I should thank you, for if it had not been for you coming along, that horse might have never gotten well."

When he was ready to leave my dad gave him a ten-dollar bill and my mother handed him a big bundle of food, enough to last him for a few days. He gave us a name and the name of his hometown, but was it true? We didn't really know who he was nor where he was from, nor where he went, and we never saw him again. There's one thing we do know. He knew how to doctor horses.

HE CURED THE MALARIA

Years later my brother Frank and I were on the bum and were jungled up under a railroad bridge, when I came down with malaria fever for the ninth straight year.

I was really sick. We had an old quilt and three old army blankets which Frank had wrapped around me, as I was sweating like a trooper and chilling and shaking so bad I was about to freeze to death.

I was just about to resign myself to an untimely death in a hobo jungle when a little skinny hobo about fifty years old came down under the bridge and spoke to us. He looked at me and said, "You really have it bad, buddy. Have you ever had malaria before?"

I said, "Yes, eight times. Every year at the same time."

He said, "I can cure you for less than fifty cents."

I asked, "Would you tell me about it? I'll try anything."

He said, "Go to any drugstore and get a dime's worth of Gum Guaiacum and half a pint of whiskey and mix the powdered herb into the whiskey and shake well. Take a swallow every hour or two until you are well. Shake the bottle each time before taking as the undissolved herb will sink to the bottom."

I was completely well within two or three days and I have never had malaria since, and that was in mid-August 1935.

I tried to give this formula to a druggist and he said, "Gum Guaiacum isn't even recommended for use in treating malaria! I can show you in the book." And he did show me what it said.

I said, "Mister, I don't care what that book says, that formula will cure malaria."

I was just trying to pass it on for the good of humanity,

for who is in a position to know more about it than a malaria victim who was cured by this very formula.

This sounds like the senseless obstinacy being exhibited today in the Laetrile argument. When will they learn that even an expert can learn from someone who actually knows?

THE FIGHT
AT THE BROOKLYN YARDS

One time when I was coming out of the Brooklyn yards of the New York Central, which is in the extreme north end of East St. Louis, Illinois, I nearly got my head knocked off for trying to help an old man. Or perhaps just because some yokel wanted to hit someone and his mother wasn't handy.

A freight was made up when I got to the yards, so I hunted up a good clean boxcar and climbed in.

A few minutes later two well-dressed young men climbed into the car, and they retired to the other end of the car without even speaking to me. This was OK, for a self-respecting hobo or tramp doesn't want a bum to get familiar enough to start calling you by your first name.

A half million hoboes and tramps have lived and died without becoming involved with a bum or anything a bum has to offer.

The train started to move out and I saw an old man with snow-white hair try to crawl in that boxcar door. My years of experience had taught me that one of the hardest things to do was to crawl up into a boxcar after the train was moving.

I told the old man to turn loose, that he couldn't make it, but he hung on. When the train reached twenty-five or thirty miles an hour his feet and legs were dragging on the ground. I pleaded with him.

"Push yourself away from the train, Dad, before you get killed."

But he hung on to the door track. I knew that he might lose his grip any second and go under the train. I sat down on the floor and asked him again. "Please, Dad, push yourself away before it is too late." He ignored my plea.

I put my left foot against his chest and shoved (not kicked) him away from the train. He rolled end over end, but he got up. He wasn't hurt, so I stood up.

One of those well-dressed young men came at me like a tiger.

"You kicked that old man off the train and tried to kill him."

I was at a loss for words, for what he said was just the opposite from the truth. Before I knew what was happening he grabbed a brake shoe key out of the door and came at me.

He hit me under the chin and lifted me a foot or two off the floor, and before I could move he hit me over the left eye with the brake shoe key. I realized that he was trying to kill me, so I went into action.

I hit this gentleman with a left hook and a right cross and knocked him up against the wall of the car. I made a dive and grabbed the brake shoe key and twisted it out of his hand. Then I hit him as hard as I could above the left ear with the brake shoe key and he almost went down, he was staggering around in the doorway and I kicked him in the side and put him out through the door. I turned to his buddy and said, "Now you SOB you get yours."

I started to hit him with the brake shoe key and he said, "Don't hit me, I'll jump off."

I said, "You had better jump, hoodlum, or I'll be happy to knock you off."

He jumped. I never heard how any of them came out, and I don't care, for I was trying to save an old man's life.

All I know is, these two bums were standing alongside the track talking the last I saw of them.

I guess it is ironic that I got hurt worse than any of the four men involved, and I have the scars to prove it.

RIVER TRAMPS
OR JOHNBOAT HOBOES

One of the most unusual and fascinating people I ever knew was a great-aunt of mine, Rose Ayers Harper. She was born and raised in the Ozark Mountains in southwestern Missouri near Eldorado Springs.

When my grandparents moved from Missouri to Vermillion County, Illinois, near Danville, Aunt Rose soon followed them to this new-found land of plenty. She soon got a job in Danville and to all outward appearances she had settled down permanently. She even adopted a homeless ten-year-old orphan named Johnnie Draper and embarked on the trying job of raising him to manhood.

Aunt Rose was a hobo and a tramp at heart, so one day without warning she told Johnnie, "Let's get an old johnboat and go down to the Mississippi River and down the Mississippi to New Orleans."

Naturally Johnnie was fascinated by the prospects of such an adventure, so he was ready to go. Within a few days she had bought a boat and a pair of oars. She bought some groceries and several boxes of shells for her rifle, and they were ready to go.

They took off down some river over there in Illinois that emptied into the Mississippi and they were on their way.

Somewhere along the line they picked up a little mangy pup and took him aboard the johnboat. Later on they found a young turkey floating down the Mississippi on a board, so they hauled it in and took it aboard.

One night they camped on a sandbar and when they awoke the next morning they found a little black chicken wandering around, looking for something to eat, so she adopted it and added it to her now sizable family of river tramps.

She had a tarpaulin that they put up at night as a pup tent to sleep in, and they usually camped on a sandbar, thus making it harder for anyone to slip up on them. The pup, turkey, and chicken slept in the tent with them.

Aunt Rose was awakened one night by the pup growling so she looked out and saw the dark figure of a man wading in the water about ten feet out from the edge of the sandbar. He would take two or three steps, then stop and listen for a few seconds, then come on. She had picked her rifle up and was sitting there watching him make his approach. When he got closer she saw that he had a shotgun in his hands.

She asked him, "What do you think you are doing, slipping up on me at two or three o'clock in the morning?"

He said, "Shut up woman, or I'll blow your head off now."

She put her rifle to her shoulder and fired. She said he fell face down in the water and never uttered a sound, and the last she saw of him he was floating down the river and finally disappeared from sight. She said she was so scared and nervous that she reloaded her gun and sat there the rest of the night watching and listening, but nothing happened.

She used to tell me, "You know Charlie, I just might have hit that old devil right between the eyes!"

Knowing her as I did, I would say that if she could see him well enough, she did put that bullet right between his eyes.

She and Johnnie and the menagerie finally arrived in New Orleans, they had taken seven weeks to make the trip of approximately nine hundred miles.

She sold the boat for five dollars and gave the man the livestock as a bonus. She and Johnnie came back on a passenger train, much richer in terms of experience.

She always praised that little pup for awakening her and thereby probably saving their lives. She was single when she made this first trip, but some years later she married an attorney by the name of Jacob Harper, and she was destined to teach Uncle Jake some new tricks.

In 1916 some of Uncle Jake's relatives died and left him $21,000. He asked Aunt Rose what she would like to do in the way of taking a vacation?

She didn't hesitate very long. She said, "I'll tell you what let's do, let's get old Graf Fox (my grandfather) to build us a new fourteen-foot johnboat and we'll load it with supplies and go down the Wabash to the Ohio and down the Ohio River to the Mississippi and down the Mississippi to New Orleans."

Since he had never heard of such a wild venture or adventure, he was ready to go. The boat was soon built and loaded with provisions and they were on the way.

They piddled along, as she said, and got drunk in every town along the river, from Terre Haute, Indiana, to New Orleans, Louisiana. As a result it took them two and a half months to make the trip. Uncle Jake said that was the most fun he ever had in his life and the greatest vacation he had ever taken.

This Aunt Rose was a character, the likes of which few of us have ever seen. I think the world would be better off if we had a few more Rose Ayers Harpers.

When they came back from New Orleans they decided to get Graf to build them a new cabin in the Wabash River bottoms. They lived happily in the cabin until the first big flood, then they had to move out, so they went back to Danville, Illinois.

The next year Aunt Rose decided that they should go down on the Wabash and spend a few weeks with Graf and Molly Fox. Uncle Jake had inherited another $11,000. They could have ridden the best train on the C.&E.I. and traveled first class, but again Aunt Rose showed her affinity for hobo-ology and trampism. She said, "Jake, let's get a good push cart and load our belongings into it and walk down there. We can camp along the way and have a real good time."

171

I have heard Granpa tell it many times and I quote, "I looked up one day and here came Rose and Jake up the towpath pushing a loaded push cart."

I was born and raised on the old Wabash and Erie Canal property so this towpath was a levee or dam type manmade ridge of dirt that the mules walked on to pull the canal boats, which were a modern mode of travel when I got there.

Uncle Jake was a graduate of Harvard Law School and the son of a wealthy New Jersey family. He fell from the good graces of society because of his excessive drinking, but he found a more enjoyable life as a tramp who had one of the greatest tutors on Earth, Aunt Rose.

THE STICK ON THE COFFEE POT

I was under a bridge one time making coffee in a half-gallon molasses bucket and my coffee kept boiling over and running out onto the ground, so I was irritated and was using a bunch of typical Fox epithets when some old hobo came down under the bridge and over to where I was.

He asked, "What's your trouble, buddy?"

I told him and he said, "If you would lay a small stick across the top of that bucket it wouldn't boil over."

I thought he was joking and told him so.

He said, "Go ahead and try it and you will see that I am not joking."

I broke a little limb off a bush and skinned the leaves off and laid it across the bucket. My coffee settled right down and I didn't lose another drop. I invited the old man to have a cup of mud with me and he accepted.

We talked and drank coffee for about half an hour and he said it was time for him to go. I thanked him again for teaching me that little trick and he left. I never saw him again, but his teaching has served me well and will be with me always.

ESSAY ON THE
AMERICAN HOBOES AND TRAMPS

In my younger days I was a little bit of everything, a hobo, tramp, and often just a plain hitchhiker. I was always whatever it took to serve my purpose and need of the moment. If I wanted to get someplace in a hurry I rode the water tank on a passenger, or the top of a manifest, or a redball freight. If I was just passing my time, I usually walked along the side of a road and jungled up for a day or two whenever I got tired and needed to rest up. When I got ready or restless I would resume my long walk to nowhere.

Usually some farmer will come out and offer you a few days' work, which most tramps will accept if the guy has anything to offer. Years ago we were happy to get an offer of a dollar a day and your board and room.

However, I have met farmers that were looking for a chump, someone to exploit. This type of character is stupid enough to think that a tramp is broke, down and out, hungry, and desperate. I never was either one of these things, even when I was flat broke and hadn't had a square meal for three or four days.

It is my personal experience and opinion that no professional tramp would ever allow himself to be exploited so by some sucker-hunting rube.

The decent honest farmer depended to a large degree on hoboes and tramps to get his crops harvested and etc. and the decent honest hoboes and tramps depended on these farmers, for even a hobo or a tramp likes to have a little money in his pocket to pay his way when he is traveling.

The average farmer years ago was glad to see a drifter come along during the busy season. It was the factory own-

174

ers or managers that made something dirty out of the word drifter. If there hadn't been any drifters there wouldn't have been any pioneer settlers in the Americas. Yes, we owe the old-time drifters a debt of gratitude, men like Daniel Boone, Jim Bowie, Sam Houston, Kit Carson, Buffalo Bill Cody and ten thousand others, the most notable of which was no doubt Davy Crockett.

All of our first ancestors in America were drifters, so people who live in glass houses shouldn't throw rocks. The only Americans that are not descendants of drifters are the blacks and the red Americans.

In all my years on the road I never dreamed that the time would ever come when people would become interested in the day to day life and experiences of the old-time hobo, but apparently that day has come. Perhaps because the true hoboes have been put on the endangered species list, and this is what stimulated an interest in the whooping crane, the bison or wild buffalo, fur seals, bald eagles and so on.

To quote the statement of a competent authority in a UPI interview in 1976, I quote, "There are less than two hundred genuine hoboes left and all but one of these men are over sixty years old." Unquote.

When we consider that there were an estimated sixty to a hundred thousand real hoboes on the road in America in the 1920s and a mere two hundred in the mid 1970s it appears that the odd job man's ranks are badly depleted.

The men that split wood, beat the carpet, mowed the lawn, painted the picket fence, and pumped the wash water for a meal of just a couple of sandwiches in a paper sack will, I am afraid, be only a memory within a few years.

The passing of the hobo will be the end of an era, of an independent race, a part of Americana. Like the Bedouins (Arab nomads) the chief desire of the true hobo is to live free and die free. Like the Bedouins who prefer to die in their tents in the solitude of the desert, the average hobo or tramp would prefer to die beside his little bonfire beneath a bridge with simple dignity and freedom.

Following are some names and phrases that were common to hoboes, tramps and railroaders in general.

A connie was a conductor. A hog mauler was an engineer. A brakey was a brakeman. A coal passer was a fireman. A steam hog was a coal-burning engine. An oil burner was an engine that was jet fired with oil or a modern diesel.

In the early days of railroading they had wood burners and wood crews ever so many miles that cut and stacked wood along the right-of-way to be picked up by the train crews. The last wood burner I saw was on a narrow gauge line in southern Arkansas, and this was close to fifty years ago.

A crummy was a caboose. A reefer was a refrigerator car. A gonnie was a gondola. A pot of mud was a pot of coffee. Toppings were pastry of any kind. Punk was bread. A grease ranch was a restaurant. The sally was the Salvation Army. A ding shop was any mission or transient camp. Dukie was anything to eat. A lump and handout is the same thing, a sack or package of food. A set down is when someone invites you into their home or place of business to sit down at a table and eat. A gump was a chicken. A sack of weed was a bag of tobacco. A pack of butts was a package of hard rolls or tailor-made cigarettes. Shooting snipes or hitting grounders was picking up a cigarette butt that someone had thrown away. Hitting a New Yorker was finding a long cigarette butt, nearly a whole cigarette that some prosperous gent had thrown away. Sinkers was donuts. A stiff was a tramp or hobo that carried his personal belongings in a bundle, often suspended from the end of a stick that he carried over his shoulder. A booster, a jug heister or a jake leg denoted a chronic drunk as a rule. There is a specific ailment that heavy drinkers get after so long a time called jake leg. A jake legger usually takes two steps with one leg while he is taking one with the other, which makes him appear to be walking somewhat sidewise.

One of the old favorites of years ago with hoboes and

tramps was the thousand-mile shirt. This was the black sateen shirt that was in style thirty-five to fifty years ago. They were popular with road men, for you could wear one a thousand miles between washings. They didn't show dirt, unless it was white dirt of some kind.

To skoff meant to eat. Kip meant to sleep, pearl diving meant washing dishes. As a road man would say, "I had to do a half hour or an hour of pearl diving for that set down."

A yard bull was a railroad detective in the yards, and a cinder dick was a detective who rode trains, and frequently rode the tops. The function of these men was to guard precious cargo, they were sometimes called shacks, they loved to get rid of hoboes.

A jungle was a hobo camp and it could be anywhere. Alongside of a railroad, under a trestle or a viaduct or under a highway bridge, or wagon bridge as they used to call them. Old deserted buildings or shanties near a railroad are often used as jungles.

A coop or a clink was a jail.

One time I met a hobo friend of mine who had two broken fingers on his right hand. He had them splinted with those flat sticks out of Eskimo Pie ice cream bars. I asked him how he broke them?

He said, "I was up there in front of the Lyric Theater the other evening shooting a few snipes when a guy and a girl came along and stopped at the ticket window. He had a cigarette that he had just lit and as he started into the show he took a quick drag on it and threw it out on the sidewalk. I bent over to hit that New Yorker and just as I took hold of it some guy stepped on my hand and broke those two fingers.

"He felt so sorry about hurting me that he gave me a five-dollar bill and said, 'Go get you some cigarettes and go to a doctor and get those fingers taken care of.'

"I went to a drugstore and got a ten-cent roll of gauze and two Eskimo Pies and two packs of cigarettes, then I went out on the street and met some tramp and got him to splint those fingers for me. I had eaten both of the Eskimo Pies and licked the sticks off good and clean, so the splinting was easy.

"When he had finished I told the tramp to go with me to a restaurant and I would buy him a bowl of soup beans, a hamburger, and a cup of mud. We went down to a little grease ranch and skoffed, and the last I saw of him that tramp was a happy man."

Most any respectable hobo or tramp is always watching out for lice of any kind, for there are filthy, slovenly people in all walks of life and all levels of society who have lice of one kind or another, chronically.

Head lice are called walking dandruff. Body lice are called seam squirrels, and crabs are called crotch crickets. But don't be misled, for crabs don't infest the human crotch only, but all parts of the body where there is any hair, including the eyebrows and armpits.

The strange thing is, in contrary to the tales you hear about hoboes, tramps and bums, I never picked up any kind of lice on the road. I had all kinds once, each. I got body lice in school when I was in sixth grade. I got crabs from sleeping on a couch where an elderly respectable housewife had lain a day or two before, and I got head lice in an orphan's home where I was working.

The best louse killer there is in the world is plain old kerosene or coal oil as it is commonly known. Put a good coating of it all over your body and let it stay on for thirty minutes to an hour, then take a bath with Castile soap if you have it, or any kind of soap that will cut grease or oil. This treatment will kill lice, nits and all at the same time.

For head lice wash your hair thoroughly with kerosene and let set for twenty minutes to one half hour, then wash your hair with a strong soap to get all the oil out. Then top it off with a regular shampoo and you are rid of the walking dandruff.

Now back to common definitions. A tanker is one of those

tank cars that everyone has seen on the railroads. They can be hauling oil, gasoline, wine, vinegar, chemicals and so on. Any kind of liquid, so they aren't the most desirable type of transportation. On many occasions I have been forced to ride them. You ride the catwalk around the lower part of the tank and ride the side of the car (or the side catwalk) but never the end of the car. Just in case something should happen.

PERSONAL HYGIENE
AND MENTAL CLEANLINESS

I learned early in my career as a hobo that you can do a lot better if you keep yourself as clean and presentable as possible at all times. Jesus pointed out that "as a man thinketh, so is it." Taking a lesson from these words I always tried to make as good an impression as possible during my years on the road.

I used to go into a barbershop about once a month and ding a hair cut and never had any barber refuse me. Sometimes I had to wait until he had taken care of all the cash customers first, which was only right and proper, but my turn always came sooner or later. I used to ding a bar of Ivory soap and I always specified Ivory laundry soap, for it is an all-purpose soap for shaving, bathing, and washing clothes, and I never had any grocery man refuse me. I have actually seen some shopkeeper run a dirty tramp out of his place of business, then turn around and ask me, "What can I do for you?" He knew I was a tramp too, but I was a clean tramp.

My buddy Jack Ross made a little device to hold a Gem razor blade and we could sharpen our blades and shave indefinitely with each blade. We sharpened the blades by rotating them against the inside surface of a drinking glass. I experimented one time with a blade using this device and got 117 shaves out of a single blade.

In those days most everyone wore cloth caps with a stiff bill, and those caps also got filthy in a short time. I used to find a bottle of some kind and wash it out and go to a service station and ding a bottle of regular gasoline, and go out to the jungle and wash my cap and lay it on a log or bush and let it dry out completely and I was ready to go again, with the same as a new cap.

So I will point out that in all walks of life, cleanliness will always be a redeeming virtue. The word cleanliness should include the whole person, for inner cleanliness is even much more important than outer cleanliness.

There is nothing more disgusting and revolting than a man or woman who looks upon every member of the opposite sex as an object of exploitation.

The majority of old-time hoboes and tramps had the greatest respect for the rights of all humanity, and I have seen thousands of them that you could trust much farther around your wife and family than you could many people who went to church and professed to be Christians. Of course there were bad hoboes, just as there are good and bad in all segments of society.

I have seen jungle retribution and hobo justice, and it is usually swift and thorough. Since hoboes have no money or worldly wealth, it is pretty obvious that most all fights and arguments must of necessity be based on some type of moral issue. I have known a good many hoboes who carried Bibles and read them daily and tried to live up to the prescribed moral standards that are stressed in some parts of the Bible, yet they had never been in a church in their entire lives. Even I recognized these people as genuinely good men.

I have been in a few hobo jungles where violent fights occurred for no valid reason. In every case the fights were confined to and started by a bunch of "rum dumbs" that were hopped up on some type of alcoholic beverage or pills of the goofball variety. One time there were thirty-five guys in a fight in the jungle at Belen, New Mexico, and most of them were drunk and troublesome, so a war started. I didn't get involved in it, but I saw the deputy sheriffs round them all up and transport them to the county bastile.

Rest assured that any decent self-respecting hobo always tried his best to steer clear of these fiascoes.

THE LAST HOBO

I sit by a little campfire alone
Beside the railroad track.
My pals have caught that westbound freight
And they won't be coming back.

We never thought when we were young
That the day must surely come
When we'd ride our final westbound freight
To the land beyond the sun.

So thought this ancient vagabond
I'm the last of a kind to be.
I've worried about this these many years;
O why did the Lord pick me?

RAILROAD LINGO AND DUTIES

When a roundhouse foreman said, "As soon as you get that K-4 ready let me know, I've got to run her east light to pick up 26," this meant that he was going to send the engine east alone, with just an engineer, fireman and a brakeman, and number 26, a passenger train had broken down and this K-4 was needed as a replacement engine to take the train on to its destination. If he said, "We are going dead head this N-2 to Columbus or Rose Lake," he meant that he was going to couple the N-2 to the back end of the engine on some train and pull the dead engine to Columbus or Rose Lake for major repairs. In this case they would open the double heading cock on the dead engine and put it on straight air so that it would operate and function the same as a boxcar or a Pullman coach would in a train. Two white flags on the front of an engine means that it is an extra or a local, and that this train will stop and set off and pick up cars at all little towns, elevators and mills along the road for a distance of forty or fifty miles, more or less, and that it will go in the hole, go on a siding for all other traffic. This is a bird dog train, for its job is to pick up loaded cars and deliver them to the nearest big yards so they can be put on a regular through freight and taken to their destination. The bird dog will set off x number of empty cars at a place and pick up x number of loaded cars that are ready for shipment.

Humping cars in a railroad yard means moving them from one track to another in order to make up trains. This is done with a yard engine, the old Pennsylvania Railroad used to use the little H-6 and ocassionally an H-10 on the hump.

When the engineer gets a car on the right track he will give the engine a little steam until he is running about ten or twelve miles per hour. Then the brakeman will pull the pin lifter and cut the car loose from the engine and let it roll slowly down the track until it bumps and couples up with its specified train.

All cars carrying explosives and such have a red sign with black letters nailed to each door that says "DON'T HUMP." It is wise to obey this sign!

During World War Two I saw a half-drunk hump engineer humping carloads of ammunition and other war materiel. They finally caught him and he nearly got sent to prison for that little stunt.

The foregoing are a few of the things one could expect to hear on the railroads years ago. This kind of lingo wouldn't mean much to the average person, but the men who were responsible for seeing that everything ran to the time schedule, these terms were all important. The old-time railroads ran by almost split-second timing. At least they tried hard to do so.

As an example, if a freight was pulling into a yard or a passenger was pulling into a depot, any railroader could pull out his watch and tell you exactly if the train was on time, or late, and how much late it was, or if it was ahead of schedule they noted that too.

TRIBUTE TO TOMMY CONNORS

I worked on various railroads in my younger days, the Santa Fe, Texas Pacific, and the Pennsylvania, and in each case I started as a gandy dancer. That is a section hand on the track gang. On the Pennsy I went up the ladder, from a section hand to a class "E" machinist. I served my apprenticeship on the Pennsy under one of the finest little Irishmen that I ever knew, Tommy Connors. Tommy was in charge of the "dead gang," or dead end of the roundhouse, as they called it.

This was where they overhauled the freight and yard engines, and this is where I became a machinist. Tommy Connors must have undoubtedly been one of the greatest teachers of all time when you consider that it takes two years to serve an apprenticeship and become a machinist, and I passed my tests with a grade of 98 and was set up to a machinist in eleven months.

When I passed my test, 250 questions, 150 written questions and 100 oral questions, I came back and told Tommy, I made it, and I remember his words to this day, for they made me feel pretty good.

He said, "No doubt ye did Charlie, for ye can learn anything quicker than any mon I ivver seen in me life."

I stayed on the Pennsy as a machinist for a few years, then one day they told me that business was falling off and I would have to bump a man named Prunner who had a wife and six children to support. I told the superintendent to get me a resignation slip and I would fill it out.

I went on the road again and Prunner kept his job. I liked the road better anyway.

THE ALL-TIME HOBO KING

One of the best known hoboes of all was Jeff Davis, the self-appointed king of all the hoboes. He was definitely one of the most popular men that ever rode the rails and one of the most eager to help anyone in need.

Once you met him you never forgot him. I have seen the initials J.D. countless times all over the country. As an example of his personal magnetism I will cite you an incident.

Jeff slept in a farmer's barn one cold night and a day or two later the farmer found the initials J.D. done in yellow crayon on the inside of his barn door and I will quote the farmer's comment about those initials. Quote: "I wouldn't take five hundred dollars for those initials, for he was the most unusual man I ever met.

"I would have liked to had a brother just like him."

Though I only met Jeff once, in the Big 4 Cafe in Matoon, Illinois, I will heartily agree with that farmer.

THE RATS WERE TOO BIG

I went into Kokomo, Indiana, one September, looking for a few days' work. In those days if you was looking for work all you had to do was go to the courthouse square and hang around awhile and someone would show up and hire you.

When I got there I asked a man if he knew of anyone who was needing a man. He said, "Yes, those Amish Dutchmen up there on the north side of the square are looking for tomato pickers."

I went up and talked to them and one guy said, "Come home with me, I've got some work for you."

He had a farm about eight miles out of Kokomo. When we got there he said, "I'll show you around and by that time my wife will have supper ready."

He had told me in town that he paid ten cents a crate for picking tomatoes and fed you and gave you a place to sleep.

He took me up in the haymow of his barn and said, "You can sleep up here in the hay, we will give you three wool blankets to keep you warm."

I went to bed in the hay about 9:00 P.M. I was tired so I soon fell asleep. Sometime later I was awakened by a heavy object lying on my face. I didn't move for a few seconds, then I felt a slight movement so I knew it was some living creature. I came up with my right hand as hard and fast as I could and knocked the unwelcome visitor off my face and sat up instantly to find out what it was. There was an open window in the end of the barn, up high and the moon was shining into the haymow through that window, and I saw a large rat scampering madly across the hay in an effort to get away from me.

Fortunately I slept for many years with the covers up over my face for various reasons, and this kept the rat from getting into a skin-to-skin relationship with me. I hollered and cursed and stamped my feet and when I finally quieted down I couldn't hear a sound, other than my own breathing.

I went back to bed and covered my head and tucked the blankets under me securely, and was stupid enough to think that I had ran all the rats out of the barn and made it a safe place to sleep. I had just started to doze off when here came two rats that must have weighed two pounds apiece, and they ran the full length of my body (on top of the blankets) and jumped off my forehead and chased each other all over that hay and were soon joined by six or eight more. They were running in all directions.

In desperation I took my blankets and went out into the open yard between the barn and the house. There were no rats out there but I spent the remainder of the night trying to keep from freezing to death. I probably got forty-five minutes sleep that night, so I was tired, sleepy and mad when my boss got up and came downstairs. He saw me standing on the back porch wrapped in blankets, so he called me in and asked me, "How did you sleep?"

I told him, "I didn't sleep."

He looked surprised and asked, "Why?"

I told him about the rats and he looked at me like I was crazy.

He said, "Oh! The rats won't hurt you."

I asked, "Did you ever try to sleep with rats?"

He said, "No."

I asked him if he had a spare bedroom and he said, "Yes, but the help doesn't sleep in the house and they don't eat at the table with my family and I."

I never wanted to whip a man so bad in my life, and didn't do it. This was supposed to be a religious man! If he was, I am glad that I am a sinner.

Then I remembered that I had ate my supper the evening before at a little square table that sat against the back wall of the kitchen, and I was naive enough to think they just didn't have enough room at the dining table. I had been eating with humans all my life, but this dingbat actually thought his family was too good to sleep in the same house or eat at the same table with a common laborer.

The sweat of laborers had given them everything they had.

I decided to pick all the tomatoes I could that day, get my money and take off before dark and before I lost control of myself and killed this egotistical fool.

I picked twelve crates of tomatoes that day so I had one dollar and twenty cents coming. I quit about 4:00 P.M. and went to the house and told him to give me my money. He said, "You did a good job and if it is warm and sunny tomorrow you should be able to get four or five crates more than you did today."

This is the reasoning of a hog!

I told him I wouldn't pick another tomato for him if I starved to death.

He looked shocked and said, "You get off my place right now!"

I said, "I'll get off soon enough but right now I wish you would lay one of your dirty paws on me so I could have a good reason to knock your chin up between your eyes."

He took off for the house and I went inside the barn and got my pack and left.

I couldn't get back to feeling like a normal human until I was a long way from there. May the Lord have mercy on any poor unfortunate person who is made a victim by such un-principled people as that man. His family seemed nice, but he dominated them completely also. I imagine they envied my freedom to tell him off and walk away.

THE IOWA KID FROM HOLLYWOOD

I was brewing a can of coffee one morning beside the U.P. yards at Sparks, Nevada, and I had a big sack of glazed donuts and little "snail" cookies sitting there beside me on the ground. When the coffee was just about done a young man came along and spoke to me. I greeted him and asked if he had been to breakfast?

He said, "No, I haven't."

I invited him to stay and eat with me and he accepted. I told him to get a bean can that was sitting nearby to drink his coffee from. When the coffee was done I rinsed out his can and mine with boiling coffee, then filled the cans so they could be cooling while we ate.

We started working on those big sinkers and snails and talking. I asked him where he was going and he said, "Home, to Iowa!"

I asked, "Where have you been?"

He said, "I'll tell the story and it is stupid, but I suppose you have heard them before. I was led to believe that I was so handsome I was a cinch to make it big in Hollywood. I fell for this line and drew all my savings out of the bank and headed for the coast. When I got to Hollywood, I found gangs of young men and women who had come out there from all over the country in the belief that they were all natural-born movie actors. A few got bit parts, but the majority of us couldn't even get into the studios to talk to anyone, much less get hired."

He went on talking. "I was bound to make it so I stayed on and on until my money ran out. I wrote home for my dad to send me a hundred dollars, and he sent it. I just kept trying day after day and before long I sent for another hundred dollars, and he sent that. A few weeks later I was broke again. You won't believe it, but I wrote Dad for another hundred dollars. He sent it, but this time he suggested that maybe I had better come home, as it didn't look like I was going to do any good out there, and he isn't a rich man. I got ashamed of my stupidity and the fact that I was a total failure, so when I got down to my last couple of dollars I decided to head for home. I have never known what it was to go without anything, so I was flat broke when I got to Fresno, and as a result I haven't had a bite to eat for over twenty-four hours."

I said, "Why didn't you mooch something?"

He said, "I couldn't do that, I thought of it but I just didn't have the nerve to do it."

I said, "Well, buddy, whether you like it or not you are just another hobo and you had better act like one if you want to get by."

He said, "I thought someone would invite me to eat, but you are the first one, and I don't know how to thank you."

I assured him that he didn't need to thank me and that it was kindly nice to have someone to eat with and talk to.

As I looked at him and thought of his story I began to feel sorry for him in spite of the fact that a faint heart never made a good hobo neither, to quote an old saying about lovers.

By the time we had finished eating, I had made up my mind, so I said, "I'm going right through Iowa, so I'll take you home and see to it that you don't go hungry."

He said, "No, I couldn't do that, that would be just too much."

I said, "You can't ding either, and you can't change my mind. I'll take you home."

He just looked at me and didn't say anything, so I changed the subject and when the next train headed east Reefer Charlie and the Iowa Kid was on it.

We arrived at his hometown a few days later and he called his dad and asked him to come into town and get us. His folks lived on a nice old farm about five or six miles from town.

The Iowa Kid had spent all his twenty-four years here except for the several months he had been in Hollywood trying
to become a movie actor. His dad came and we went out to
the farm.

On the way home Iowa told his dad all about me and what
I had done for him.

The old man took a shine to me and said he wanted me to
stick around for a while, so I accepted his invitation and
said that I would stay with them for a few days.

I had been there three or four days when he asked me
why I didn't change my mind and stay with them permanently. He said, "I've raised eight kids, five boys and three
girls and I would like you to join us and become one of the
family."

I said, "I'll tell you like your son told me in Sparks, Nevada, I couldn't do that, but I have a reason, I am a hobo
and I get jittery when I'm not traveling.

"You might say, a rolling stone gathers no moss, but remember this, a setting hen lays no eggs so if I have a choice
I'd rather be a rolling stone."

I stayed a week and one morning I heard an old steam
train whistle and I was ready to go. Those that haven't been
there can't realize the magnetic force and attraction that an
old steamer's whistle had for the hoboes of long ago.

I kind of hated to leave these good people, but they had
their lives to live and having a stranger in the house is
bound to create some problems.

I picked up my pack and shook hands with all of them
and they were still begging me not to go. The old man pulled
out a twenty-dollar bill and tried to put it into my hand, but
I made it plain that I didn't want it and wouldn't take it. He
put it back in his billfold and took out a "fin" (five-dollar
bill) and crammed it down into my shirt pocket and said,
"Now, Reefer, if you don't take that we won't let you leave."

I said, "OK, thank you."

The old lady had me a nice lump fixed up, fried chicken
and biscuits and half a raisin pie. Old hobo movie actor

buddy Iowa put his arm around my shoulders and said, "I'll never forget you, come back and see us."

For one reason or another I never managed to get back to see them, but I want to say this, Iowa, if you are still living and remember the Sparks Donut Man, write to me. I would like to hear from you.

THE DRUNK IN THE CASKET

When I was a kid the old Vandalia Railroad used to go through Terre Haute, Indiana, and there were a good many business places along the sides of the railroad.On the north side of the track there was a casket factory between 6th and 7th streets, and this had been a busy place before the Depression came along. They shipped hundreds of boxcar loads of caskets annually to various parts of the country. By 1933 they had become just another victim of Hoover's prosperity period. They went bankrupt and laid off all their employees permanently and closed their doors forever. Within two years the windows were all knocked out and the doors were standing open, so the hoboes and tramps started using the building as a flophouse.

In 1935 I was sitting up there in the old casket factory one rainy day, talking to some old hobo buddies of mine, when in came four rum dums all boozed up, and they had two quarts of cheap whiskey which they were hitting at regular intervals.

They spoke to us and sat down on the floor about thirty feet from us. Finally one of them stretched out on the floor and passed out.

The tables and wooden horses that had been used to build caskets on were still sitting there, as well as three or four casket shells that had not been finished.

They were most likely defective in some way. The rummy that was passed out had been sleeping serenely for about an hour when his buddies decided to have some fun with him. They picked him up and laid him in one of the old casket shells and hunted up a lid shell and placed it on the coffin.

He was out about another hour, then we heard him mumbling and cursing inside the casket. He finally

194

knocked the lid off onto the floor and we heard him say, "Hey! Where the hell am I?"

He raised up on one elbow and felt of the outside of the coffin with his other hand. Then he felt of the inside and said, "Jesus Christ, I'm dead and I've been dead a long time for the lining is all gone out of my coffin."

He was so drunk and worried about being dead that he didn't even see any of us nor hear us laughing at his antics.

He finally tried to get out of the coffin and fell on the floor, cursing wildly. We heard him say, "I'm getting out of here. They never built a graveyard that could hold me."

Then he jumped up and ran staggering for an open door. He missed the opening and ran into the door facing and almost killed himself. He laid there on the floor for a minute or two and was about half sober when he got up that time, so he looked around and saw his buddies sitting there laughing and asked, "What happened and how did I get here so fast? A minute ago I was somewhere in a graveyard?"

They all talked the situation over, but they didn't tell their buddy what really happened. They drank some more whiskey and one by one they laid down and fell into the deep sleep of the just and were all sprawled out on the floor resting comfortably when I left.

By the time this event took place the "Old Van" was gone, for the Vandalia Railroad Company had sold out to the Pennsylvania Railroad Company. They went broke and merged with the New York Central (Big 4) and became known as the Penn Central and they didn't make it so Conrail was born. This company soon failed and was absorbed by Amtrak and there is no assurance that it will last any great length of time. The old Van and the old Pennsy were much better railroads for a lot less money.

OLD SHANTY TOWN

Back in the late 1920s and all through the 1930s and
1940s there was a place on north Third Street in
Terre Haute, Indiana, called Shanty Town which
was owned and operated by a man named George Warner
and his wife, Laura. The Warners were very nice people and
consequently very well thought of, at least by the poor
people of that area.

During the years that Shanty Town was in existence I
imagine there were at least five thousand hoboes and
tramps made their home there off and on, not to mention
the thousands of poverty-stricken Terre Haute citizens who
always came back to Shanty Town when the going got too
rough.

The Warners had five little one-room cabins and two fairly
large homemade house trailers that were usually occupied
by people with children. The cabins and trailers were furnished with all the necessary equipment to live comfortably. The cabins rented for four dollars a month and you
could pay by the week or by the month as you chose. The
trailers were five dollars a month, or a dollar and a quarter a
week.

When the weather got bad and I was in the Terre Haute
area I always went to see old buddy George and got a cabin
to hole up in until spring. Even though times were hard
you could always come up with a buck for the rent and
twenty cents for two bushel baskets of lump coal to heat
your cabin for another week. You could go down on Main
Street and make that much money shaking hands.

I usually found three or four odd jobs a week and if all else
failed I could always go down to some gym and pick up a
buck or two helping train and work out amateur boxers, re-
pairing equipment or whatever etc.

196

I got a steady job one winter delivering corn whiskey and sugar mule (cut alcohol) for a local bootlegger to the sporting houses in the red light district on Terre Haute's famous or infamous west side. This special order stuff delivered retailed for a dollar a pint and I got twenty-five cents of that buck for making the delivery. Providing whiskey for the girls' customers was a paying business in those days.

If I delivered twenty pints in a day I made five dollars and that was a young fortune at that time.

I used to take a market basket full of pints and half-pints out to the Trianon Ballroom at 29th and Main on dance nights and peddle them to the "tailor-made suit element." Now and then I would sell out early and have to call the boss and have him bring me another basket of joy juice. These were the nights! I used to make some big money on those dances.

I even had two well-known doctors that I made regular deliveries to twice a week.

I was doing well as a walking rum runner, but I was always afraid I would get caught, so when the sun began to shine and the first warm breezes caressed my face, I headed for the railroad yards with a roll of long green as big as my wrist and caught the first train out. As I sat in the boxcar and listened to those wheel flanges clicking against the rails I knew that I must be the happiest man alive, for I didn't have a worry in the world. I was totally free and financially secure, and that long open road was ahead of me.

The very poor and the wanderers don't have any Shanty Towns to go to anymore when they are in a tight spot and want to stay free while they try to make it on their own.

Today your burden is made substantially heavier by a lot of preconceived bureaucratic rules and regulations that allow the aged and infirm to be picked up and confined in some institution type hacienda so some fast buck hustler can turn in a bill against the government for services rendered. This is pure snologlotomy (horse manure).

Old age, sickness, and death are a natural sequence to

life, as established by the Creator, and neither of them are an invitation to nor conducive to exploitation by anyone.

This is why the old-time hoboes for the most part preferred to die with dignity, as a free human are your natural rights. Since the human animal is by nature a wanderer, I am amazed that there aren't more hoboes and tramps than there are good people.

JEFF CARR

One notorious railroad dick in the Union Pacific yards at Cheyenne, Wyoming, used to ride his big white horse alongside a train and knock any bo that he could reach off the train with his two-foot-long hickory club and hopefully kill him. If he saw a bo riding the top of a train he would try to shoot him off with his revolver.

Consequently old Jeff killed a lot of men during his years at Cheyenne. The law of the inevitable finally caught up with him, he tackled the wrong man and they found old Jeff lying alongside the track shot full of holes and beat to a pulp with a piece of iron, and the killer was never caught.

Jeff was killed in 1925 and I didn't hit the road until 1929, so I was spared the misery of a confrontation with Mr. Carr! The memory of old Jeff lived on for many years in the hobo jungles and rail yards all across the country. As the saying goes, quote, "He had put the fear of God in hoboes far and wide."

Cheyenne was bad enough in my years on the road, for there was a "bull school" there and there were twenty-one young railroad dicks on duty there in the U.P. yards, so you caught or got off trains on Sherman Hill two miles west of Cheyenne.

There were two kinds of railroad detectives, the cinder bulls who were stationed at a specific railroad yard, and the shacks who rode certain trains over a specific division, usually one hundred miles between division points. A lot of division point dicks never bothered hoboes as long as the bos were just passing through. They were concerned with wanted men and God knows there were enough of them.

The jack-rollers, escaped convicts and murderers were a constant threat to the bos in more ways than one. Jack-rollers were anything; in the areas of holdup men, pick-pockets, burglars, muggers and so on.

There were always a lot of would-be hoboes wherever you went. All they were or ever would be was a bunch of crude windjammers and nothing more. Aside from the multitude of self-styled hobo kings, you met quite a few "super hoboes" who tried to convince you that they never underwent any of the common everyday problems and hardships that were an integral part of the everyday life of the real hoboes.

One good example of a super bo was a fellow that showed up at the annual hobo convention at Britt, Iowa, some years back. He said he had been a hobo for x number of years and had never did anything but ride freight trains and pointed out that he had never hitchhiked, nor did any walking along railroads nor highways and had never asked anyone for anything.

Anyone that would tell such a tale couldn't know much if anything about hoboing, for any real bo has done all these things ten thousand times if he was on the road for any length of time.

My old friend "Hobo Bill" Mainer asked me what I thought about this tale.

I said, "He never was a hobo nor any other kind of a road man or he would have done all these things many times."

Hobo Bill used to say, "Everybody has to serve his apprenticeship as a bum and as a tramp before he can qualify to be a genuine hobo."

This is true, for I spent a lot of hard miserable days and nights as a bum when I was a teenage boy and also many days and nights as a tramp walking the highways and by-ways, taking a lot of guff from a lot of people.

Bums and tramps sleep in halls, doorways and on the steps of empty buildings and eat at any mission they happen to find or hear about. These are the true "mission stiffs."

They have no purpose, ambition, nor hope. As "Colum-

200

bus Eddie" O'Brion used to say, "They are the scum of the earth!"

The true hobo doesn't have a permanent home and doesn't want one, but he does have a purpose in life, for his is hunting a job so he can pay his way. As long as you refuse to give up you will never be beat.

Like all segments of society there were a few bad hoboes, but by and large the majority of real bos were fairly honest and dependable.

Many people think the world owes them a living, nonsense, the only thing the world owes you is a chance. It is up to you to make your own living.

As proof of what I'm saying, consider the natural creatures of the fields and forests. Many of them gather and store food when it becomes available in preparation for the barren days ahead. This is one of the most important laws of survival. This is their God-given chance. Not that He owed them a living per se, but from the beginning His plan was to give all His creatures a chance to survive.

SURVIVAL

The key word in the life of any hobo or tramp was survival, for this concept was an integral part of every hour of every day of life on the road. Those who didn't learn the art of survival usually wound up dead or maimed for life.

Getting on or off of a moving train was a very dangerous undertaking if you didn't know the right way to do it!

Always get on or off the front end of a car. Front means the way the train was going. If you tried to grab or get off the back end of a car and lost your balance or your hold on the grab iron you would most likely fall between the cars and get cut up like hamburger.

Countless thousands died or lost arms or legs by making this mistake. Another no-no was sitting in the door of a boxcar on a moving train and letting your legs and feet hang down. We have all been tempted to do this, for it is pleasant to just sit there and watch the countryside gliding by. It is too dangerous, for your feet can get caught on a switch dolly or any object lying along the track and jerk you out on the ground or even under the train. Either way you would get badly hurt or killed! Some states had laws that prohibited sitting in boxcar doorways, and a violation of this law was good for ten to thirty days in jail if they caught you.

HOBO COOKERY
AND TRICKS OF THE ROAD

For the most part, hoboes had to make the most of whatever they had on hand, or what they could get hold of, so they invented some unusual meals, most of which were pretty tasty. One of my favorites was salmagundy. You mixed several things together and fried the whole shebang until it was done then add a little water and let it boil for five or ten minutes and you have a meal fit for a king. Be sure to season any food with salt and pepper to taste. Follow these steps and you will come out OK:

Cut three or four slices of bacon into pieces about one-half inch long and fry it crisp. Peel and dice potatoes and an onion or two and dump them in the skillet with the bacon and bacon grease. Stir well and let fry to a crisp brown. Then add a raw egg or two and stir until the eggs are done and thoroughly mixed with the other ingredients. Adding or not adding water is optional.

Another good cheap meal can be made by frying your chopped bacon and diced onion together, then add a can of red or kidney beans and let boil for a few minutes and your meal is ready.

This chopped fried bacon and diced onion enhances the taste of most boiled or fried vegetable foods. This fried bacon and onion will give hominy, canned spinach or any fresh greens a much better taste. The fact that hoboes and tramps always cooked on a campfire had a lot to do with making food taste better.

Even a pot of soup beans are much better when cooked on an open fire, and a pinch of cayenne pepper will make them even more tasty. Don't forget the ever-present need for enough salt to kill that wild taste found in beans of any kind.

Let us not forget the all-time hobo special, Mulligan stew. Following is my stew recipe, for each hobo had his or her special way of making Mulligan, and each thought their way was best. I never saw any bad stew, except the one can with the whole calf head eyes and all looking up at me through the stew.

Here is a stew recipe that will please most people:

Take four or five quartered or diced potatoes, two medium onions diced, one teaspoon of fresh garlic chopped or like amount of powdered garlic, two or three carrots cut into one-half-inch chunks, two or three celery sticks cut in small chunks, one cup of chopped cabbage, one small can of tomato sauce or two or three ripe tomatoes cut up, one can of yellow hominy or can of corn or fresh corn cut off the cob, one can of red beans or kidney beans. Meat of any kind cut in small chunks, or hamburger or pork sausage torn into small pieces. To this point I have described just plain old vegetable soup, but the hobo idea of seasoning changes that concept.

Put one teaspoon of thyme, one teaspoon of powdered or fresh dillweed or dill seed if you can't do any better, one-half teaspoon of cayenne pepper or a small red chili pepper cut into small pieces

The hobo king Steam Train Maury Graham has had better luck when he added a dash or two of soy sauce to his stew. The recipe above will feed five or six hungry people. You can cut the amounts of ingredients or increase them, depending on how many you plan to feed.

204

THE ROAD DOGS OF LONG AGO

Many bos and tramps were fond of dogs, so it wasn't too uncommon to meet a bo or a tramp with a canine companion. A dog of any size would give you security and friendship and permit you to get a good night's sleep without having to sleep with one eye open. These dogs were roadwise in every respect and a good judge of human character. They wouldn't allow the wrong people to get too close to their human road buddy. Hood River Blackie used to tell the story of an old bo called Bullfrog Blackie and his little dog.

Quote: "Bullfrog Blackie got off a freight train in Indianapolis, Indiana, and was walking up the street with his pack on his back and his little dog walking beside him. They hadn't gone far when two cops stopped them and arrested Bullfrog for vagrancy. They took him to jail and his little dog to the dog pound. Bullfrog immediately started complaining about them taking his dog away from him. The complaint became so heated that the news of what started the trouble finally got to the county prosecutor's office. Being a dog lover himself, the prosecutor ordered the chief of police to release Bullfrog Blackie and his dog at once and let them go on their way with no further molestation. Needless to say, Blackie was grateful to that prosecutor the rest of his life."

Bullfrog Blackie was born and raised on a farm near Terre Haute, Indiana, but spent most of his life on the West Coast, picking fruit and working the harvest fields in general. I've never met anyone who knew Bullfrog Blackie's right name; but that doesn't matter much, for he was well known and well liked all up and down the West Coast, and that is the important thing.

According to his story, he was engaged to a beautiful

Indiana farm girl back in 1898, but before they could get married she got sick and died.

He was heartbroken, so he hit the road and was a hobo until his death in 1979. The last few years of his life his friends had to help him up into and down out of boxcars wherever he went, but he kept riding freight trains.

Every hobo and tramp I ever knew or heard tell of had some kind of a story of why they chose to become a vagabond. I don't think there was ever such a thing as a natural born hobo nor tramp.

My story was a very common one and so simple. My family broke up when I was three months and seventeen days past my fourteenth birthday and I hit the road twenty-one days before my fifteenth birthday and was on the road almost constantly until I was age twenty-five, then intermittently until I was age thirty-six. I have done considerable traveling since 1946 as a rubber-tired hobo, meaning I traveled by cars and trucks, riding the cushions as we used to say.

An old lady adopted me when I was eighteen and a half years old and treated me wonderfully, but she could never understand me. After sleeping in boxcars on concrete slabs and the bare ground for so long, I didn't feel comfortable in a bed. She used to come in to get me up to eat my breakfast and I would be rolled up in a blanket beside the bed with my shoes for a pillow.

She did washings and ironings for people to make her living, and I gave her half the money I got hold of. In addition to this meager help I kept her in coal all winter. I used to grab a coal train at night and throw half a ton or ton of nice block coal off and haul it home with a borrowed pushcart and put the coal in her shed.

None of us were thieves in the strict sense of the word, but you would be a little silly if you went hungry or cold in a land of plenty. Considering that you aren't shorting someone else to supply your needs.

Those were hard cruel years, but we survived, and this was the name of the game. During the Depression years of the 1930s, many people chose or were forced to become involved in all sorts of crime. But as strange as it might seem, we have perhaps fifteen times as much crime of all types today as we had in the Depression years.

Today the unemployment figure is 7 percent, whereas in the 1930s unemployment reached a high of 35 to 50 percent depending on the locality. Some even higher!

Most of today's crime appears to be based on a vicious rebellion against social order in general. In the Depression years the criminals hid from society, but it is the exact opposite now, for society has to hide from the criminals.

Jails are no longer the only places with bars on the windows and doors and the bolt lock and gun businesses are booming.

Hoboes had all sorts of gimmicks to find work in various states and it was important to know the places to go if you expected to find work.

One place I'll never forget was the big hobo jungle beside the Milwaukee main line at Mitchell, South Dakota. I've seen as many as a thousand to fifteen hundred men there at one time, all looking for work in the harvest fields. And believe it or not, all those men would be working within a week or ten days. It is very important for the farmers to know where they can pick up one or a dozen men on a moment's notice. For when that grain is ready to harvest you can't put the job off for three or four days and expect to get a bumper yield when one-fourth of the grain is lying on the ground having been shelled out by a gentle breeze or perhaps a strong wind. Hoboes had many ways of making a living, and some were highly skilled individuals.

Sharpening knives, scissors and saws was a lucrative trade. Painting and lettering mailboxes was another good gimmick. If you knew how to mix, pour, and finish concrete steps, walks etc., you could usually find all the work you could do.

I knew an old bo from Coopers Falls, New York, Ed Smodell, who had a diamond-studded profession. He was a master at building circular stairways. Ed only wanted two or three stair jobs a year and he could live like a king and not be tied down to nobody, nowhere.

When I first met Ed Smodell, I thought he was a college professor or a retired senator, but he straightened me out in a hurry with a few words. He said, "Let's hunt up a good jungle and I'll cook a big pot of stew. I've got all the fixins except the meat!"

Being an old stem worker I said, "I'll get the meat and meet you back at the jungle by the time you get the fixins in the can."

That was the beginning of a real good long-time friendship. Ed finally married some old maid whose folks had died and left her a lot of money and 250 acres of farmland. Ed built a new house on the land and let some farmer farm the place on the halves, so their living was assured.

Ed and his wife lived together about three and a half years and got along like two kittens. They never had a harsh word. Then Ed got pneumonia and was dead within twelve hours. I went to visit her a couple times after he died and she made my heart ache, for she was the loneliest human I ever saw. I came down from Michigan two or three years later and she had died some months before. Someone found her dead in bed, so I assume she had a heart attack.

I met four or five piano tuners on the road and the ones that wasn't drunks seemed to always have a little money to live on. There were quite a few house carpenters (both rough and finish carpenters) and they could usually find all the work they wanted. People tend to criticize drunks, but as long as they don't mix drinking with their work I don't see too much wrong with their way of life.

I have known many men that wouldn't take a drink all week, but come Friday evening they got drunk and stayed drunk until Sunday night. This is what you call controlled drinking. On the other hand I have known quite a few men who never took a drink in their life but spent at least half their life in prison for committing some hon-sencical crime, for no good reason.

There were many problem drinkers and these were the worst kind, for just one-half pint of cut alcohol (white mule) could keep them on a two or three weeks' drunk. At fifteen cents a pint, you could stay drunk for a long time for five or six dollars. The better grade of whiskey (homemade corn whiskey) was twenty-five cents a pint or two dollars a gallon. There is a lot to be said for corn whiskey, for that was the only whiskey ever made that wouldn't make you sick nor give you a headache, no matter how much you drank. Neither did it ever cause you to get on one of those "nutty runnin drunks," as they used to call them.

Men or women with no home, no family, and very little hope were always candidates for the college of drunkology, consequently the hobo legions had their share of drunks. Most of them were friendly and peaceful, but now and then you would find an agitator as in all segments of society. You didn't fool around with these dudes. You just hit him hard and fast and escorted them out of the jungle camp and sent them on their way.

Many hoboes could play harmonicas and Jew's harps, so we used to sit around the campfire in the evening and play and sing old railroad songs until midnight or until we got sleepy. I spent many happy evenings taking part in these jam sessions.

Speaking of music in the hobo jungles, you could expect anything. I met an old Polish fellow who was an accordion player and a good one! You never knew what song he was playing, for the only songs he knew were Polish folk songs and classical music. I've met men that could get music out of two teaspoons and five or six glass bottles with varying amounts of water in each bottle. There were many "rattle bones" players, the greatest of whom was no doubt Steam Train Maury Graham. I've heard Steam Train accompany two professional bands with his rattle bones and Jew's harp and he gave those bands a special quality that I will long remember.

Piano players were quite numerous but were at a disadvantage, for you couldn't carry a piano around with you.

The best piano player I ever saw was a little drunken bo named Frankie Stegner. He had studied piano playing in France under the old masters when he was young. For some unknown reason he became a chronic drunk and spent the last years of his life playing in honky-tonks for two dollars a night and a couple of hamburger sandwiches.

I met a guy in St. Joe, Missouri, that had made a musical instrument out of a piece of broom handle and one guitar string (a G string I think), he had cut a notch in one end of the stick and bored a hole through both sides of the notch to accommodate a guitar key so he could adjust the string tension. He had a piece of a guitar bridge glued into a crosswise notch near the back end of the stick. Naturally it wasn't as good as a guitar, but he could play several songs well enough that you could recognize the melody.

Steam Train Maury is still on the road and has camped along many riverbanks and in any woods that happens to appeal to him and enhance his endless quest for spiritual and physical freedom. One of the greatest assets to wilderness camping is the feeling of closeness to the Creator. Nowhere else is this feeling so evident.

210

HOBO HISTORY

I will conclude this book by mentioning the names and miscellaneous information and comments on a few of the old-time road men that were on the road before 1930. I will exclude the degenerates, and the criminal element that were quite numerous before 1930. For they contributed nothing to the true hobo society per se. Their main reason for mixing in with the hobo legions was purely and simply for the obvious protection of anonymity, on trains and in the hobo jungles.

The word "jungles" was a term used to identify the countless hobo camps that were all over the forty-eight states, in the U.S. at that time.

Many of the old-time genuine hoboes were celibates, and it was from this segment of the hobo legions that the code of the road came into being. This was a simple code of ethics that was adhered to by the majority of genuine hoboes. Men who lived by the code could be and were trusted by their employers and their wives and children. Many farmers have to be gone from home for a day or two or maybe a week now and then, so it was a great relief to be able to trust their employees.

We always had a few self-styled lover boys in every group of hoboes, but they didn't fare too well as a rule.

The main code rule was morality i.e. keep your hands off and thoughts and remarks to yourself regarding all females, particularly married women. Many would-be Romeos lost a lot of skin off his head for violating this rule, for such violation would eliminate the possibility of getting work or a handout for all bos that came along in the future.

One of the greatest misconceptions regarding hoboes is the public's idea about a total lack of hobo hygiene, for nothing could be farther from the truth.

The genuine hobo bathed, shaved, and washed his clothes in creeks, rivers or lakes any time the need arose and thereby kept himself looking presentable.

Common sense would tell you that the typical cartoon character type hobo would be a cinch to get picked up by the police in any town. Moreover what housewife would get close enough to hand such an obnoxious character a handout, much less invite him into her home for a set down. They wouldn't even let him mow the lawn nor hoe the garden!

In the days of the real hoboes you could go into the Salvation Army or a Goodwill Store and invest three or four dollars and come out looking like the duke of Macaroni.

Even if you were broke and had to ding some shoes or clothes, they would always give you something better than you came in with.

The only time I could ever afford to wear Florsheim shoes, Hart-Schaffner and Marx suits and Stetson hats was when I was on the road and doing all my shopping at the Goodwill Stores. Since I became a home guard I've never been able to afford such luxuries. Any good hobo had a system of survival that he could count on when he was broke. It is not as hard to get by on the road as one might think. It is all in knowing how. Your appearance and initial approach to a potential benefactor are the key factors. Other important factors in dealing with the public are planting the seeds of honesty and sincerity. Never try to fast talk anyone, for they will get suspicious of you. This is where the gypsies and a lot of salesmen make a bad mistake in believing that everyone is a sucker or a chump.

I met the first hobo I had ever seen, as far as I know, when I was nine years old. His name was Noah Pennyleak and he was a native of Canada. Noah wound up in Terre Haute, Indiana, in 1922. About six months after he arrived, his son and grandson came into Terre Haute from somewhere and decided to stay for a while. They were unusual people, for old Noah had made himself a steady job shortly after he got

212

to Terre Haute by rounding up four or five pool halls to clean up a couple times a week.

His son Alonzo was a genuinely good handyman, for he could repair anything from furniture to bicycles and kids' toys and even picture frames. All the tools he had were a screwdriver, a pair of pliers and a small ball peen hammer. Alonzo never wanted for work, for he was busy most of the time. He was teaching his son how to repair things, for this trade was a good gimmick for a road man.

The second hobo I met was "Smokey Joe" Evans in 1924. Smokey Joe was a master concrete finisher and was hired by my dad who was a construction boss for Fouts Construction Company in Terre Haute, Indiana.

Joe mentioned that he would have to find a place to board and room and my dad brought him home that evening and he stayed with us about six months. Typical of the old-time hobo, he soon endeared himself to us and became just like one of the family. But the day finally came when he said, "I've stayed in one place long enough, I've got to hit the road again for a while, so I'll be taking off in a few days."

That was a sad day when he picked up his suitcase and told us good-bye. I never saw nor heard of him again until 1934. I went into Tulsa, Oklahoma, and was walking down Main Street (Route 66) when I saw a sign that said, "Smokey Joe's Pool Room." Out of curiosity I went in to see if it was the Smokey Joe I knew, and it was! I stayed a few days with him by invitation, and we were a couple of happy people.

He shoved some paper money in my pocket when I left and asked me to come back, but I never saw him again.

In 1979 I asked a West Coast hobo pal of mine, "Hood River Blackie" Gooding, if he knew Smokey Joe?

Blackie wrote back and said, "Yes, Joe's a pal of mine, when Joe retired from construction work and from the road, he bought a little cabin in Gila Bend, Arizona, and he's living there now. I go down to see him five or six times a year and I'll tell him you was asking about him."

Joe would be in his late nineties if he's still living, so I imagine he's caught the westbound (died).

In 1932 I met a young man at the Southern Pacific fruit sheds at Modesto, California. He was introduced to me as John Fisk and we spent three or four days there, trying to get a job sorting and packing fruit. I finally gave up in disgust and caught an eastbound fruit express on the U.P. bound for Chicago.

This Fisk kid made an impression on me and I never forgot him. A lifetime later I heard of an old bo that went to the hobo convention in Britt, Iowa, every year who was known as "Fry Pan Jack" Fisk. I inquired if this Fry Pan was really John Fisk of Seattle, Washington and got an affirmative answer.

I got some gratifying news in August 1984, to wit: Fry Pan Jack was elected king of the national hoboes. I'm sure he will be a good hobo king, for even as a seventeen-year-old kid he had a lot of common sense and the courage to back up his convictions.

Another old bo that I traveled many miles with was "Neck Bones Shorty" (Mungo Penman) of Mattson Furnace, Pennsylvania. Mungo was known as "Sarge" Penman by many bos because he was a retired master sergeant out of the army and had served in both the Spanish American War and also World War One. He was quite an old road man and would back a friend regardless of the odds.

When I was campus welder for Indiana University Medical Center at Indianapolis back in the 1960s, I got a big surprise. We maintenance men ate our lunch at two big tables in the Tin Shop. I noticed that some sixty- or sixty-five-year-old man always sat across the table from me and every time I would look at him he would smile at me.

I finally asked why he kept smiling at me all the time?

He said, "You don't know me, do you?"

I said, "Your face is familiar, but I can't place you."

He said, "I've sat by many campfires and drank coffee out of tin cans with you."

214

Right off I said, "You must be an ex-hobo."

He grinned and said, "Don't you remember old Sioux City?"

I said, "Charlie Drake."

He said, "That's what's left of me."

The other men got a bang out of this revelation, so from then on every noon hour was hobo history hour.

"Sioux City" Charlie Drake was one of the finest humans I ever knew. I don't think he ever had a hot argument or a fight with anyone in his life.

This is indeed unusual, for 90 percent of the old bos had been to Fist City anywhere from a few to many times. And arguments were frequent and heated as a rule. So Sioux City Charlie would have made a good buddy for Jesus, but even Jesus went on the warpath one time and threw all the money changers out of the temple.

Charlie died in the late sixties but I will never forget him.

THE SUN-DOWN GANG

The sad part of this whole story is nearly all my old road buddies are gone to that big jungle in the sky. I often think of them and a terrible loneliness possesses me.

Hood River Blackie used to say, "I don't want to be the last hobo!" I agree with Blackie for neither do I want the dubious distinction of being the last of a breed of individuals of any kind.

One of the most unusual hoboes of all is a hobo of world-wide renown, Frisco Jack as he is known to millions of people the world over.

Frisco merits the respect of not only the hoboes but nearly every segment of society, and this is a wonderful example for any individual to set. At the National Hobo Convention at Britt, Iowa, in August 1985 Frisco Jack was elected national king of the hoboes, and I am sure he will be a good king.

The most unusual hobo king to date is Steam Train Maury Graham, for he was elected king five times and had to refuse to run for a sixth term or he might have become a permanent fixture in the highest office a hobo can hold.

Steam Train is a natural born pusher and promoter and could sell an anchor to a drowning man or a straw hat to an Eskimo. By virtue of his public appeal and use of words he has become a very widely known individual.

Steam Train has appeared on many TV programs and has gotten scores of writeups in various magazines and newspapers.

One of his favorite pastimes is visiting hospitals, nursing homes, prisons, senior citizens' centers and anywhere else that he thinks a visitor and a few kind words would give these folks something to live for.

In appearance, he is a dead ringer for the fictional character Santa Claus. In every respect and as a consequence he is in great demand at shopping malls to entertain the kids during the Christmas season in the great malls of his hometown of Toledo, Ohio. A few years ago when dope of all kinds began to invade the schools, he hit the campaign trail and lectured many hours on the evils of narcotics.

In my opinion this was a very worthwhile effort, for I am sure a lot of youngsters heeded his words and benefited from his efforts. If he saved only one child, his time wasn't a total loss!

Another great ex-hobo was my dear friend John "Rambling Kid" Moxie of Staunton, Virginia. John got into the concrete business back in 1939 and by 1960 he had become a very wealthy man. As strange as it might seem, John's wealth didn't go to his head, as the saying goes, on the contrary, it was a means of making him become a great humanitarian.

Naturally, his family came first, but he never passed up a chance to help someone in need. He was such a great human that I could write a whole book on the generosity of John Moxie the Rambling Kid.

A family member said, quote, "John gave away over one million dollars in the last fourteen years of his life." There aren't many John Moxies in this world. The average human views money in terms of affluence and power and a solely self-serving commodity. I'm sure the Rambling Kid has been rewarded for his good deeds in the land beyond the sun.

John was a religious man seven days a week and that alone would win him a goodly number of points I am sure.

John owned the Staunton Braves baseball team and so it was that he had to go to Lakeland, Florida, in March 1981 to attend a baseball executives meeting. The meeting adjourned about 11:30 P.M. March 24 and John went to the parking lot to get his car. As he was unlocking his car door someone slipped up behind him and hit him in the head

217

with something and robbed him. He was found lying beside his car unconscious the next morning and taken to a Lakeland Hospital and was later taken to Staunton, Virginia, and died three days later without regaining consciousness. As far as I know the killer was never caught. John's untimely end came as a terrible shock to all who knew him.

During my years on the road I met countless thousands of men, many of whom I never really knew and some that I didn't want to know.

I met a hobo from Brooklyn, New York, who refused to do any type of manual labor. His clothes and shoes were worn out, and about the only food he got was what some tenderhearted bo gave him. The first thing he did every morning was get out and mooch or steal a newspaper and the only thing he ever read was the stock market report. This dude was obviously playing with a short deck.

Euell Gibbons used to say, "There are two things that I will never be and that is a mission stiff or a skid row bum." You can get ever so low and poor but if you will keep a little pride you will make it some way. The skid row district in any big city was something beyond belief. We used to call these big city slums the concrete jungle.

Little Chuck Lehman used to call these slums the valley of lost souls.

I want to make one point clear, this is where you separate the genuine hoboes from the bums and tramps! It wasn't that the hobo was superior to any other type of vagabond, it was just that the true hobo kept trying and the tougher it got, the harder they tried.

These derelicts of the concrete jungle were surely and simply committing mental suicide.

When I hit the road in the 1920s the self-assumed elite of the hobo jungles was the Pete men or safe blowers. They kept to themselves as a rule but were congenial and as a rule quite generous and courteous, so long as you minded your own business. They despised anyone that tried to ask them a lot of personal questions, justifiably so, for even a preacher would be offended if you asked him a lot of personal questions. The Pete men called these nosy people yokels and rubes. If there was ever any honor among thieves it had to apply to the old-time Pete men, for they had a code of ethics that they lived by and it was inflexible.

Many a man has been badly hurt or even killed for violating this code.

I imagine all the old Pete men are long dead, but as in all cases I must assume, some other criminal element soon took their place.

I have tried to locate some of the old hobo jungles here in Indiana but without much success. Everything has changed drastically in the last forty years and not always for the best.

A hobo didn't have to be provoked into quitting a job, if they got itchy feet they just took off and wasn't mad at anyone. The freedom of the open road and the lack of responsibility were powerful inducements to accept and love an otherwise hard and dangerous way of life. Every noise of a freight train and the long lonesome whistle of an old steam engine was more than a true hobo could resist for any length of time.

As Hood River Blackie used to say, "The whistle of a steam engine was the most beautiful music ever created by man."

In spite of a hobo's desire to be free, he was endowed with a sense of duty to himself and to society, in the context that he wanted to provide for his daily needs, whenever and however he could.

This desire for self-sufficiency was why we would travel a thousand miles if need be to get a job in the harvest fields, or on a railroad section gang, or on any kind of a job that would pay a living wage.

There was nothing glamourous nor romantic about the life of a hobo, but it was educational, if you had a receptive mind. The Rambling Kid, John Moxie, has told me many times, quote, "I thank the good Lord for giving us the courage to endure and survive the hardships that we went through during those bad years!" I concur heartily, John, for we were down many times but we were never out.

Most people beat themselves by negative thinking. As the Bible says, "As you think, so is it." This is a true statement.

A very good, long-time hobo friend of mine was Adam Roscoe "Soldier" Fields of Terre Haute, Indiana. Soldier was put in the Glenn Orphan's Home at Terre Haute when he was only a few weeks old and completely deserted and forgotten by his legal parents, whoever they were.

The only identification ever was a note that was pinned to his gown when someone at the home found him lying on the front steps of the administration building. He was raised at the home until he was twelve years old, at which time he ran away from the home. World War One was just starting and since he was more mature and looked older than his years, he joined the army and was soon sent to France. Three or four months later he was in a front line trench during a big battle and the Germans were really shelling those trenches. All of a sudden Soldier started laughing. The man next to him asked what he was laughing about?

Soldier said, "This is my birthday. I'm thirteen years old today."

His trench buddy said, "Hell, you are just a kid! What are you doing over here?"

Soldier told the man to not say anything about it. But as soon as they fell back to a rest area the man reported the situation to the commanding officer and he had Soldier brought to his tent. After a few questions he said, "I don't want any kids here, so you are going to go back to the States on the first thing going that way."

When Soldier got back, he was immediately discharged. Having no home nor family, he headed for the nearest hobo jungle and became a hobo and roamed the country in boxcars until he was age eighteen. He re-enlisted and was sent to Panama for seven years, during which time he became a boxer and eventually turned professional and in the ensuing years he racked up 285 pro fights.

When he was discharged the second time he went right back to the boxcars and toured the country, picking up fights wherever he could until he got too old. Then he got into construction work and followed that until he retired.

In 1940 he married some young widow in Coolidge, Arizona, where Soldier had been for some time, working on the Coolidge Dam project. He and his wife came to Terre Haute to see me in April 1940. His wife had just bought him a new Olds four-door sedan as a present, so he wanted me to meet his new (only) wife and see his new car. We had a nice visit, and that was the last time I ever saw him.

In the late seventies I wrote to Hood River Blackie and asked if he knew where Soldier Fields was. Blackie wrote and said, "Yes! When Soldier retired, he bought a little shack near the dam and has become a home guard."

So I assume Soldier's wife must have died or divorced him between 1940 and 1978 or '79. About three weeks later Blackie wrote and said they had to take Soldier to a hospital in Prescott, Arizona, as he was in a bad shape from emphysema and wasn't expected to live long. A few days later he wrote and said Soldier had died. I'll miss him as long as I live.

Hood River Blackie died January 30, 1984 from a series of ten heart attacks over a three-week period. He died in Twenty Nine Palms, California, at the High Desert Medical Center. I'm sure Blackie will be missed by many people from all walks of life, for he was an unusual man in many ways.

He was the official hobo historian of America and a talented writer of hobo lore. He made many hours of tapes of hobo history for Harvard University and also for the California State Museum in Sacramento.

Blackie was also a poet of remarkable talent. He had written records of over six hundred hoboes, and these records are in his long-time friend and attorney's office in Ukiah, California.

Hood River Blackie (Ralph Gooding) was born August 5, 1926 in Marion, Ohio, to a sixteen-year-old unwed high school girl. In those days they took an illegitimate child away from the mother and put it in an orphanage shortly after it was born. So it was that Blackie spent several years in the orphanage, namely, until he got big enough to work. Various farmers took him out of the home for short periods of time, until he was fourteen years old, the year was 1940. Some farmer that he was helping at that time lost his temper and threw a pitchfork at Blackie and the show was over. Blackie packed his clothes and left. He caught a freight train and headed west. He entered the world of the hoboes and found some real friends, which was a totally new experience to him.

When the hoboes heard the story of his life, they more or less adopted him and took care of him until he was old enough to take care of himself.

One of Blackie's favorite expressions was, quote, "I never had a mother, but I had a thousand fathers."

As a young man Blackie became a friend of an old hobo by the name of "Tex" Meadors who had been on the road fifty-one years at that time and was seventy years old, but still riding trains and working in the harvest fields and so on.

Blackie and Tex traveled together for years until Tex was in his nineties, at which time he decided he was getting too old to catch trains any longer so he checked into a nursing home in Seattle. He soon tired of nursing home life and ran away. The people at the nursing home called the police, and the hunt was on. They found old Tex in a nearby railroad yard, trying to climb up into a boxcar. He was soon back in the nursing home and was an angry and disgusted old man. Tex died in his ninety-sixth year and is buried in Yuba City, California.

Tex and Blackie had bought a double lot in the Yuba City

Cemetery years ago so they could be buried side by side. But since Blackie decided to be cremated, I'm not sure how their previous plans came out.

Hood River Blackie wasn't a run of the mill hobo in any sense, for he had more tricks than a dog has fleas! He used to worry all of us from time to time by getting killed by a train. About the time we had decided that poor old Blackie had finally caught the westbound, he would show up somewhere and we knew we had been hoodwinked again.

After years of worrying and wondering, we finally found out what he was actually doing and how he was able to fool so many people. Unlike most hoboes, Blackie had a bad habit of buying a lot of things on credit, knowing that he would never be able to pay for it. When he got head over heels in debt and his creditors were hounding him, he would get killed again and the bills were paid, or at least crossed off the books.

His method was so simple that he fooled a lot of people. Being a professional writer and a master with words, he used his little portable typewriter to free himself of unpaid debts.

He would hole up for a few days and type up an obituary in great detail and sign the name of some columnist to it and mail it to some paper two or three hundred miles away and they would print it and never suspect that it was phony.

Other papers would pick up the story and within a few days it was known far and wide. Then Blackie would hop a freight at night and disappear into Arizona for five or six months. When people quit thinking and talking about him he would show up in some remote town in California, Oregon, or perhaps Omak, Washington.

In spite of Blackie's unorthodox ways he was generally well liked by most people, though he was unpredictable for the most part.

Nevertheless, he deserves the benefit of the doubt, for if all of us had to live the way he did, from the cradle to the grave, we would have no doubt been worse than he ever was!

There was an old Indian saying, quote, "Never judge anyone until you have walked two miles in their moccasins."

About twenty years ago (1965) Blackie started writing a hobo book from notes that were the true day to day history of over six hundred hoboes.

Like twenty-five or thirty other bos I've known, he didn't live to finish the book.

I am certain that it would have been one of the greatest books of its kind that was ever written. The greatest published book on hoboes to date is *Knights of the Road* by Roger A. Bruns. Several ex-bos have written some good small books on their personal experiences on the road, most of which were very interesting and gave John Q. Public an insight into the life of a hobo, but if you stick with actual facts, it cuts down on your volume. Even so, that is better than cutting down on the quality of your work.

In conclusion let me say I hope this book has given you at least a little enjoyment, and more importantly that it gave you a clear view of both sides of the picture. The day of the hobo is gone, perhaps forever. It is logical to assume that a new breed of tramp will evolve out of all this confusion, and when this happens I hope they conduct themselves as well as the old-timers did. Good principles, good morals, and integrity will get you by wherever you go, even though you are flat broke and ragged. These three things established a great image for Jesus in spite of the fact that he had very few clothes and no money and no work, and there are no Roman soldiers to nail you on a cross because they disagree with your philosophy.

I would not recommend a life on the road as a panacea for all your worldly problems, but I will say this, if you are a good person at heart and conduct yourself properly, this life will be conducive to achieving a state of mental peace that is seldom possible in the ranks of conventional society.

MAINLINE SLIM

The old hobo stood by the water tower,
His vision growing dim.
Who would think this ancient man
Was the famous Mainline Slim.

He had rode the rails for forty years,
His days were almost done,
But in his time he'd rode them all,
Wherever high steel run.

He'd rode the blinds and water tanks
Of the fastest trains of all,
The Golden Arrow of the Santa Fe
And the Wabash Cannon Ball.

The famous Empire Builders diesel tank
Across the mountains high,
The little 500 of the old Northwestern
That did everything but fly.

The C.&E.I. Dixie Flyer
On down the L. and N.,
From Louisville to the southern coast,
The scourge of high iron men.

The Pennsy's Jeffersonian,
The Spirit of St. Louis too,
The Burlington's Northwestern limited
And the crack trains of the Soo.

The sea board's Golden Comet
To the fabulous land of the sun,

Passed a thousand hideous chain gangs
As she made her Gulf Coast run.

He thought of the friends of his younger days,
He'd traveled with them all.
No jungle could hold them very long
When they heard a steamer's call.

They caught them as they were pulling out
And left them on the fly,
To avoid the bulls in the depots and yards
And their ever-watchful eyes.

Most of his friends are long since gone
To that jungle in the sky.
Slim thought of friendships strong as steel
And a tear came to his eye.

He'd no doubt die by a little fire
In a lonely jungle camp,
A free man yet, a smile on his face
As the Lord snuffs out his lamp.